COMPACT *Research*

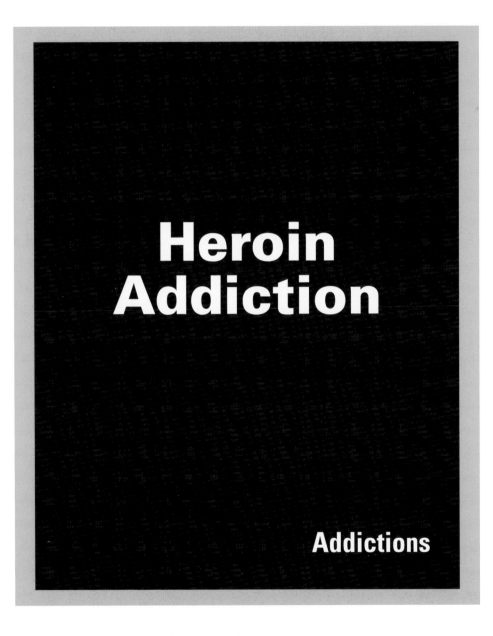

Heroin
Addiction

Addictions

ReferencePoint
Press®

San Diego, CA

Other books in the Compact Research Addictions set:

Gambling Addiction
Internet and Social Media Addiction
Sex and Pornography Addictions
Synthetic Drug Addiction

*For a complete list of titles please visit www.referencepointpress.com.

Heroin Addiction

Peggy J. Parks

Addictions

ReferencePoint
Press®

San Diego, CA

© 2015 ReferencePoint Press, Inc.
Printed in the United States

For more information, contact:
ReferencePoint Press, Inc.
PO Box 27779
San Diego, CA 92198
www.ReferencePointPress.com

LIBRARY OF CONGRESS CATALOGING-IN-PUBLICATION DATA

Parks, Peggy J., 1951–
   Heroin addiction / by Peggy J. Parks.
     pages cm. -- (Compact research series)
   Audience: Grade 9 to 12.
   Includes bibliographical references and index.
   ISBN 978-1-60152-756-1 (hardback) -- ISBN 1-60152-756-X (hardback)
  1. Heroin abuse--Juvenile literature. 2. Drug abuse--Prevention--Juvenile literature. I. Title.
   HV5822.H4P38   2014
   616.86'32--dc23

                                        2014024369

Contents

Foreword

As modern civilization continues to evolve, its ability to create, store, distribute, and access information expands exponentially. The explosion of information from all media continues to increase at a phenomenal rate. By 2020 some experts predict the worldwide information base will double every seventy-three days. While access to diverse sources of information and perspectives is paramount to any democratic society, information alone cannot help people gain knowledge and understanding. Information must be organized and presented clearly and succinctly in order to be understood. The challenge in the digital age becomes not the creation of information, but how best to sort, organize, enhance, and present information.

ReferencePoint Press developed the *Compact Research* series with this challenge of the information age in mind. More than any other subject area today, researching current issues can yield vast, diverse, and unqualified information that can be intimidating and overwhelming for even the most advanced and motivated researcher. The *Compact Research* series offers a compact, relevant, intelligent, and conveniently organized collection of information covering a variety of current topics ranging from illegal immigration and deforestation to diseases such as anorexia and meningitis.

The series focuses on three types of information: objective single-author narratives, opinion-based primary source quotations, and facts and statistics. The clearly written objective narratives provide context and reliable background information. Primary source quotes are carefully selected and cited, exposing the reader to differing points of view, and facts and statistics sections aid the reader in evaluating perspectives. Presenting these key types of information creates a richer, more balanced learning experience.

For better understanding and convenience, the series enhances information by organizing it into narrower topics and adding design features that make it easy for a reader to identify desired content. For example, in *Compact Research: Illegal Immigration*, a chapter covering the economic impact of illegal immigration has an objective narrative explaining the various ways the economy is impacted, a balanced section of numerous primary source quotes on the topic, followed by facts and full-color illustrations to encourage evaluation of contrasting perspectives.

The ancient Roman philosopher Lucius Annaeus Seneca wrote, "It is quality rather than quantity that matters." More than just a collection of content, the *Compact Research* series is simply committed to creating, finding, organizing, and presenting the most relevant and appropriate amount of information on a current topic in a user-friendly style that invites, intrigues, and fosters understanding.

Heroin Addiction at a Glance

Heroin Defined

Heroin is a powerful, addictive narcotic that is a member of a family of painkilling drugs known as opioids.

Seriousness of Problem

Mental health agencies and hospitals across the country have seen a dramatic surge in heroin use over the last two decades.

Addiction

The addictive properties of heroin make addiction a likely outcome for about one-fourth of heroin users.

User Profile

Today's heroin addicts include males and females, often in their mid-twenties and Caucasian, from suburban areas; this is a radical change from the typical heroin addicts of years ago.

Gateway Drugs

Research has shown that the majority of heroin addicts abused prescription painkilling drugs before switching to heroin.

Warning Signs of Heroin Abuse

Symptoms may include needle marks on arms and legs from repeated injections, weight loss, eyes with a dazed look, disheveled personal appearance, and noticeable personality changes.

Health Risks

Health problems associated with heroin addiction include everything from collapsed veins and serious infections to heart disease and HIV infection from using dirty needles.

Overcoming Heroin Addiction

Treatment can help heroin addicts recover, but they need to remain vigilant because of the high risk of relapse.

Overview

Ben Cimons first started experimenting with drugs when he was in middle school. Now in his early twenties, Cimons admits that he was willing to try most anything back then—except for heroin. He associated the drug with shooting up, and he wanted no part of that. "I hate needles," he says. "I can barely handle getting a flu shot." Marijuana became Cimons's drug of choice, and by his junior year of high school he was "high almost all the time."[1] Finally, after being suspended from school twice and busted for marijuana possession and distribution, Cimons knew he needed help. He spent forty-five days in a residential treatment program where he learned about addiction and gained tools that could help him stay clean.

Cimons was able to stay drug-free for more than three years. He enrolled in college, worked as a swim coach, and began thinking about a career in criminal justice. Things were going well until he started missing old friends from his drug days, whom he had intentionally been avoiding. Before long Cimons had slid back into his old habits and started getting high again—but this time there was one important difference. His drug of choice became heroin.

A Destructive Path

Cimons first tried heroin in November 2012 while at a friend's house. Some people were injecting it while others smoked or snorted it, and one of them offered some to Cimons. Since snorting was an option, he decided to give the drug a try, and he liked how it made him feel. Soon he was snorting heroin on a regular basis. A few months later, despite his aversion to needles, Cimons took someone's advice and tried shooting up. He was amazed at the effects, as he writes: "The minute it hits you, all your worries disappear. You are content with everything. You feel warm. You can't help but smile. You feel free."[2] Cimons soon learned that feeling "free" with heroin was a dangerous delusion; in fact, he became a slave to it. "Once you start injecting heroin, you can't go back," he says. "Your life becomes a bottomless pit. You no longer recognize yourself, and you can't crawl out of it."[3]

> Natural opioids are derived from opium poppies, most of which are grown in Afghanistan.

In September 2013 Cimons nearly died from a heroin overdose. He was ready to quit using until withdrawal symptoms became unbearable, and he started shooting up again. The experience proved to be a turning point, however, and within a few weeks he realized he had had enough. He was sick of being a slave to heroin and tired of living a miserable life. He spent a month at a rehab facility and then transferred to a long-term recovery house. As of May 2014 he was doing well, with high hopes for a better future.

What Is Heroin?

Many people who get hooked on heroin and then try to stop using it have a similar struggle because it is a powerful, addictive narcotic. According to the National Institute on Drug Abuse (NIDA), an estimated 25 percent of regular heroin users become addicted to it. Addiction, as defined by the NIDA, is a "chronic relapsing disease caused by changes in the brain and characterized by uncontrollable drug-seeking no matter the consequences."[4]

Heroin is part of a family of painkilling drugs known as opioids (also called opiates). The family includes natural opioids (derived from plants) and synthetic opioids (made in laboratories from chemicals). Natural opioids are derived from opium poppies, most of which are grown in Afghanistan. After the colorful flowers blossom and the petals drop off, the small seedpods grow rapidly and are harvested for the gooey sap contained within them. This is raw opium, which is used for both legal and illicit purposes. For example, it may be refined into morphine for legitimate painkilling use by doctors and hospitals. Or the morphine may be sold for use in an illicit laboratory to create a semisynthetic opioid called diacetylmorphine—better known as heroin.

> **Heroin is called by a number of street names, including crank, horse, Big H, skag, hell dust, junk, and smack.**

Heroin is called by a number of street names, including crank, horse, Big H, skag, hell dust, junk, and smack. Most heroin sold on the street is in powder form and ranges in color from off-white to brown. The color variation is caused by filler ingredients that are mixed (or "cut") with heroin in order to bulk it up. These additives may include everything from sugar, cornstarch, and powdered milk to talcum powder, dirt, other drugs, or poisonous substances such as strychnine. Black tar heroin, which is so named because it is black and sticky like roofing tar, gets its dark color from crude processing methods that leave behind impurities. According to the NIDA, most black tar heroin is produced in Mexico and is sold in US regions west of the Mississippi River.

How Serious a Problem Is Heroin Addiction?

Heroin is less common in the United States than other illicit drugs such as cocaine and especially less so than marijuana. But the heroin problem has been growing, and this is alarming to health officials and addiction experts. According to a 2013 Substance Abuse and Mental Health

Services Administration (SAMHSA) report, 467,000 Americans twelve years of age or older were regular users of heroin in 2012—which is a striking increase over 1993 when the number was 68,000. There has also been a spike in first-time heroin users over the past decade. SAMHSA data show that 156,000 people aged twelve and over used heroin for the first time in 2012, up from 90,000 in 2006. "The impact of heroin use is felt all across the United States," says the NIDA, "with heroin being identified as the most or one of the most important drug abuse issues affecting . . . regions from coast to coast."[5]

One area of the United States where heroin abuse has become a crisis is Long Island, New York. Hundreds of people have died from heroin overdoses in the past several years, shattering the region's previous records. Jeff Reynolds, who is executive director of the Long Island Council on Alcoholism and Drug Dependence, has seen a sevenfold increase in patients since 2009, and 80 percent of them have been hooked on heroin or other opioids. "We probably could have prevented most of those overdoses, through prevention, access to treatment, recovery support," says Reynolds. "Yet we didn't. So each one is an indictment of what we failed to do. But it also should energize us to say we need to get serious about this disease."[6]

Shattered Stereotypes

Americans are often shocked to learn about the heroin problem on Long Island because the users are white middle- to upper-class teens and young adults. They do not fit what is assumed to be the typical junkie profile: lower-income males, usually minorities, living in rundown urban neighborhoods. That assumption, which is widespread, is largely why Americans were so taken aback when actor Cory Monteith died from an accidental overdose in July 2013. Most people were not aware that the thirty-one-year-old star of the popular television show *Glee* had struggled with substance abuse since he was a teenager. When he died, they were saddened as well as shocked because he did not fit their idea of a heroin addict.

Today, people are starting to realize that the past junkie stereotype no longer holds true. Males and females of all ages, ethnicities, and walks of life are getting hooked on heroin. They live in rural areas and the suburbs as well as cities and no longer resemble society's perceptions of heroin addicts. "Heroin today is an urban thing and a suburban thing," says FBI

Cory Monteith, the thirty-one-year-old star of the television show Glee, *died from an accidental heroin overdose in 2013. Many people were shocked by his death, partly because he did not fit the stereotypical image of a heroin addict.*

director James B. Comey. "It's a black and white thing, a rich and poor thing. It's everywhere and everybody."[7]

Gateway Drugs

Research has shown that a major factor in the climbing heroin abuse rate is its link to prescription drug abuse. In recent years it has become increasingly common for people to migrate to heroin after experiencing the euphoric effects of prescription painkillers like hydrocodone (Vicodin) and oxycodone (OxyContin). These drugs, both of which are synthetic opioids, are prescribed by doctors for legitimate medical uses, such as easing chronic pain. But people who get hooked on opioids must often resort to buying them on the street, and the drugs are extremely expensive—sometimes as much as fifty dollars per pill. In contrast, heroin is a fraction of the cost and readily available. "Law enforcement and treatment officials throughout the country report that many heroin abusers began using the drug after having first abused prescription opioids," says the Drug Enforcement Administration (DEA). "These abusers turned to heroin because it was cheaper and/or more easily obtained than prescription drugs and because heroin provides a high similar to that of prescription opioids."[8]

One study that examined the connection between prescription painkiller abuse and heroin abuse was published in August 2013 by SAMHSA researchers. They found that four out of five first-time heroin users (about 79 percent) had previously abused prescription pain medications. This sort of finding comes as no surprise to David Mundy, whose best friend died of a heroin overdose in February 2014. Following his friend's death Mundy created a website to raise money to help the family with funeral costs, and he was flooded with text and Facebook messages from others who had lost a loved one to addiction. "Parents telling me their kids have problems, kids telling me their friends have problems," says Mundy. "We started talking to people we knew and they were doing heroin, too. And for every single one, the correlation was OxyContin."[9]

The Brain on Heroin

Although scientists have learned a great deal about addiction over the years, many questions remain about the specific mechanisms by which drugs such as heroin affect the brain. It is now known that when someone uses heroin, a complex chemical process takes place in the brain. The heroin is converted back into morphine, which then attaches to nerve cells known as opioid receptors in the brain, brainstem, and spinal cord. When opioid receptors in the brain's reward center are stimulated, this causes the release of artificially high levels of dopamine, which is known as a "feel-good" chemical. Says the NIDA: "The consequences of activating opioid receptors with externally administered opioids such as heroin . . . depend on a variety of factors: how much is used, where in the brain or body it binds, how strongly it binds and for how long, how quickly it gets there, and what happens afterward."[10]

Seconds after a user injects heroin, he or she feels a surge of euphoria known as the rush. This is typically followed by the "nod," a dreamlike state during which the user alternates between being awake and drifting off to sleep. People who are addicted continuously seek the initial rush and are obsessive about wanting that feeling back. But after prolonged use of heroin the euphoria fades into memory; the body adapts so that more and more heroin is needed just to feel normal again. The NIDA's Jack Stein explains: "Drugs hijack the brain, and you stop feeling the pleasure of the experience. The addict who used to feel great, now is lucky to feel a little better."[11]

Signs of Addiction

The symptoms of heroin abuse and addiction can vary widely from person to person depending on the type and dose of heroin, how it is used, and how users individually react to it. According to the addiction recovery organization Narconon, one of the "many sad things about heroin addiction" is that the addicts are seldom aware of how much harm they are doing to themselves. The group writes: "They will often begin to neglect their own needs, the acquisition of the day's dose of heroin being far more important. They may not eat properly and may look haggard if heroin abuse is prolonged or heavy."[12]

Along with deterioration in personal appearance and hygiene, common signs of heroin addiction include dramatic weight loss, pupils in the eyes that appear tinier than normal, and a dazed look as though the person is daydreaming. Also, heroin addicts often have a runny nose, as though they have a perpetual cold. "One reason for this," says Narconon, "is that heroin has a tendency to suppress the immune system, with the result that the body cannot fight off infections as easily and may always

Using a lighter and a spoon, an addict converts heroin from a powder into a liquid. In its liquid state, heroin can be injected. Addicts also smoke and sniff heroin in powder form.

be somewhat sick."[13] An obvious sign of heroin addiction among those who inject the drug is track marks on the arms and/or legs from needles. Often, heroin addicts attempt to hide these marks by wearing long shirts and pants at all times of the year, even during the warmest weather.

What Are the Health Risks of Heroin Addiction?

People who regularly abuse heroin can cause significant damage to their health, risking everything from sexual dysfunction and clouded thinking to abscesses (boils) on the skin and bacterial infections of the blood vessels. Referring to heroin, the Foundation for a Drug-Free World writes: "The effects on the body from continued use of this drug are very destructive. Frequent injections can cause collapsed veins and can lead to infections of the blood vessels and heart valves. Tuberculosis can result from the general poor condition of the body. Arthritis is another long-term result of heroin addiction. The addict lifestyle—where heroin users often share their needles—leads to AIDS and other contagious infections."[14]

> " An obvious sign of heroin addiction among those who inject the drug is track marks on the arms and/or legs from needles. "

Addiction experts say that regular heroin users can do severe damage to their vital organs, such as the lungs. When people use heroin their lung function slows, which is why most overdose deaths occur. "In fact," says Narconon, "a person may stop breathing before the heart stops beating."[15] Also a risk among heroin addicts is heart diseases such as infective endocarditis. This is an infection of the inner lining of the heart that is caused by bacteria spreading through the bloodstream and attaching to areas of the heart. Narconon writes: "Autopsies sometimes show clumps of bacteria growing on the valves of the heart. It is difficult for the body to reach and fight bacteria in these locations."[16]

Playing with Fire

Addiction experts say that it is very common—and extremely dangerous—for heroin users to mix the drug with alcohol or other drugs. Columbia University neuroscientist Carl L. Hart writes: "Only about a quarter of the thousands of heroin-related deaths each year occur as a result of heroin alone. The vast majority of heroin-related deaths—a whopping 70 percent or more—are caused by combining heroin with another sedative, usually alcohol."[17] This is actually what killed Monteith in July 2013. The autopsy showed that he injected heroin and drank champagne on the night of his death, and this proved to be a toxic combination.

> " Addiction experts say that it is very common—and extremely dangerous—for heroin users to mix the drug with alcohol or other drugs. "

Equally as dangerous as mixing heroin with alcohol is using the drug in combination with other drugs. This led to the accidental overdose death of a twenty-four-year-old man from New Jersey. John Hroncich, who was a third-year law student at George Washington University School of Law, had been taking an amphetamine known as Adderall while also shooting up heroin. He died at home on December 20, 2012, from what the autopsy later said was an "acute intoxication due to the combined toxic effects of heroin and amphetamine."[18]

Can People Overcome Heroin Addiction?

Countless addicts have learned that when heroin becomes a driving need, the idea of living without it seems unbearable. Some may desperately want to beat the addiction, but the fear of living without it is too much for them to bear. Those who do enter treatment go through a detoxification phase and often take certain types of drugs that can help wean them from heroin and reduce withdrawal symptoms. Following detox, heroin addicts typically participate in one or more types of psychotherapy. Through therapy they learn to understand the underlying issues that led to addiction, which helps them heal and begin to rebuild their lives.

One of the greatest risks for recovering heroin addicts is relapse, which is extremely common even after years of being clean. "Even after a long period of time," says NIDA scientist and lecturer Ruben Baler, "those trenches that addiction has been digging for years are very difficult to completely cover up; they're always there, hidden. We've stopped talking at this point in terms of curing addiction, but of just managing it on a chronic basis."[19]

What Can Be Done About Heroin Addiction?

Drug addiction is a problem that has an impact on not only the addicts themselves but their families, their communities, and ultimately the entire country. This is true of heroin addiction, which has significantly increased in prevalence in just a few decades. NIDA director Nora D. Volkow says that it will take a wide range of measures to address this problem, such as public education campaigns, widespread prevention programs, and research that focuses on the science of addiction. Also crucial is greater awareness of addiction as a medical condition that affects the brain, which Volkow says is "essential for large-scale prevention and treatment programs that require the participation of the medical community."[20]

Volkow and other experts emphasize another tactic that they believe will more effectively address America's heroin problem: focus more on treatment than punishment. Treating heroin addiction as a crime does little to alter behavior. "By engaging in a continuing therapeutic process," says Volkow, "individuals can learn how to avoid relapse and withdraw from a life of crime."[21]

Future Uncertainty

For many reasons, a drug that was once rare among the general population is growing in prevalence, and that means more people are becoming addicted. In pursuit of the coveted high, people snort, smoke, and inject heroin, often multiple times each day—and whenever they do, they are gambling with their health and their lives. Help is available for heroin addicts, but they have to want it, and their desperate need for the drug can seem impossible to overcome. With improved public policy, expanded education and prevention programs, and research that sheds light on the mysteries of addiction, the current heroin problem may start to diminish in the coming years.

How Serious a Problem Is Heroin Addiction?

66There's more heroin being used than at any time in our history. I mean, historically, heroin used to be thought of as mainly an inner city drug. That has dramatically changed, particularly over the last 10 years.99

—Neil Capretto, medical director at the Gateway Rehabilitation Center in Pittsburgh, Pennsylvania.

66Among young adults and teens, heroin use is out of control. And nobody is doing anything about it.99

—Manny Alvarez, a physician who serves as senior managing editor for health news for Fox News.

On April 16, 2014, a national summit on illegal drugs was held in Washington, DC, and a primary focus of the discussion was America's heroin problem. Police chiefs and police commissioners from throughout the United States took part in the event, as did top federal law enforcement officials including US attorney general Eric Holder, FBI director James B. Comey, and DEA administrator Michele M. Leonhart. Comey stressed how heroin abuse is affecting the entire country. "In my seven months on the job as director," he said, "I've been to 25 of my field offices, and in every single place I've visited, whether it's Mississippi, California, or Ohio, I've heard about heroin."[22]

Holder also spoke of America's widespread heroin abuse, calling it a "public health and public safety crisis." To underscore the severity of the problem, he shared a disturbing statistic with the group: Between 2006 and 2010 heroin overdose deaths in the United States increased 45 percent. Holder also explained that the rising incidence of heroin abuse is directly linked to a spike in the abuse of prescription opioids. "This staggering rise," he said, "is a tragic, but hardly unpredictable, symptom of the significant increase in prescription drug abuse we've seen over the past decade. And it has impelled law enforcement leaders to fight back aggressively."[23]

From Pain Pills to the Needle

The relationship between abuse of prescription painkiller drugs and heroin is an issue of grave concern to health officials, addiction experts, and law enforcement professionals across the United States. Research has clearly established that a strong link exists, as Leonhart explains: "We have this exploding prescription drug and heroin problem. In the body and the brain, there's no difference between taking an opiate in pill form and shooting heroin. Either way, you can become an opium addict. . . . And the reason you're seeing this on the streets in your communities is that people switch to heroin because it is cheaper and more easily available than prescription opiates on the street."[24]

The heroin/prescription painkiller abuse link was the focus of a study led by addiction expert Theodore J. Cicero, who is a psychiatry professor and vice chairman for research at Washington University School of Medicine. Published in the May 2014 issue of medical journal *JAMA Psychiatry*, the study examines two factors related to heroin abuse: how user demographics have changed over the past twenty years, and whether these changes have resulted from people switching to heroin after becoming addicted to prescription painkillers. The published report states:

> In recent years, there have been a number of mainstream media reports that the abuse of heroin has migrated from low-income urban areas with large minority populations to more affluent suburban and rural areas with primarily white populations. . . . Part of this increase in heroin use and apparent migration to a new class of users appears to be due to the coincidental increase in the abuse of prescription opioids over the last 20 years, arguably accelerated by the release of OxyContin in the mid-1990s.[25]

To conduct the study, Cicero and his colleagues analyzed data from surveys and interviews involving nearly twenty-eight hundred adults. All had been clinically diagnosed with addiction of either prescription opioids or heroin, and all had sought treatment. The researchers gathered information about each person's gender, race/ethnicity, and age of first drug use, as well as which opioid (prescription painkiller or heroin) had been abused. As the study authors write: "Respondents indicated in an open-ended format why they chose heroin as their primary drug and the interrelationship between their use of heroin and their use of prescription opioids."[26]

> "Many [communities] that had little or no heroin-related problems in the past are suddenly gripped by an unprecedented public health crisis."

By the conclusion of the study it was clear that the demographics of heroin users and addicts had changed dramatically over the past few decades. Respondents who had begun using heroin in the 1960s were primarily young urban males, African American and Caucasian, who began using heroin while in their teens. In contrast, 90 percent of heroin users who started on the drug more recently are white males and females, typically in their mid-twenties, with three-fourths being from less urban areas. Another important finding of the study was that more than 75 percent of the more recent heroin users started abusing prescription painkillers before they ever tried heroin. "In the past," says Cicero, "heroin was a drug that introduced people to narcotics. But what we're seeing now is that most people using heroin begin with prescription painkillers such as OxyContin, Percocet or Vicodin, and only switch to heroin when their prescription drug habits get too expensive."[27]

A Nationwide Problem

As reports of heroin addiction and overdose deaths have continued to mount, this has created a difficult struggle for communities throughout the United States. Many that had little or no heroin-related problems in the past are suddenly gripped by an unprecedented public health crisis. In a 2014 article, Associated Press journalist Andrew Welsh-Huggins writes:

In and around Cleveland, heroin-related overdoses killed 195 people last year [2013], shattering the previous record. Some Ohio police chiefs say heroin is easier for kids to get than beer. In Missouri, admissions to treatment programs for heroin addiction rose 700 percent in the past two decades. In Massachusetts, state police say at least 185 people have died from suspected heroin overdoses in the state since Nov. 1 [2013], and the governor has declared a public health emergency.[28]

To examine America's growing heroin abuse problem the Associated Press conducted an investigation during the spring of 2014. Journalists queried state health departments, medical examiner offices, and law enforcement agencies in twenty-six states to compile statistics about heroin use, overdose incidents, and treatment. Although several states were found to have few changes, most reported that heroin has become a significant public health concern. New Jersey, for example, is suffering from a severe heroin problem that continues to grow worse. In Camden County, New Jersey, chief of police Scott Thomson says that overdose rates have increased 91 percent in the past twenty-four months. "Because of the demand for heroin," he says, "many of the cocaine dealers are trying to broaden their own market to include heroin, which has spurred gang violence for us. At the rate I am going this year, I will have more kids from suburbia die on my streets with a syringe in their arm than inner-city youths dying from gang violence."[29]

> **Although several states were found to have few changes, most reported that heroin has become a significant public health concern.**

Tough Times in Minnesota

Another state that is struggling with an escalating heroin problem is Minnesota. The Associated Press investigation revealed that 4,519 people in the state were treated for heroin abuse in 2013—a *hundred times more* than the 450 heroin abuse cases reported in 1993. In Anoka County, which has a population of 340,000, the heroin situation has reached the crisis stage. Fifty-five people in Anoka County have died of heroin-related causes since 1999. Although one other Minnesota county had fifty-eight heroin-related deaths during that same period, its population is more than three times greater than Anoka's. "It hit us in the face in the form of dead bodies," says Dan Douglas, who is a detective with the Anoka County sheriff's office. "We didn't know how bad it was until it was too late here in our community."[30]

Like so many other communities across the United States, Anoka County's heroin problem is closely tied to prescription drug abuse. Douglas says that when he first began supervising a county task drug force in 2009 heroin was not really a concern. Then officers began to notice a steady rise in pharmacy robberies and were often finding Percocet and OxyContin when they made routine marijuana busts. After federal and state law enforcement began clamping down on illegal distribution of prescription opioids, the heroin problem in Anoka County began to soar.

> **New England has long been known for its charm and beauty. But in recent years the region has become known for something else: a devastating heroin problem.**

One Anoka County resident who died from a heroin overdose was Tanner Pap, a twenty-one-year-old student at the University of Minnesota. An athlete who had graduated from high school with honors, Pap had dreams of pursuing a career as a psychologist and drug counselor. Until he died on November 9, 2012, neither family members nor college roommates had any idea that he used heroin or any other drugs. His mother was shocked as well as devastated at the loss of her son. "I thought my suburban, middle-class family was immune to drugs such as this," she says. "I've come to realize that we are not immune. . . . Heroin will welcome anyone into its grasp."[31]

Crisis in New England

Heroin problems are gripping communities all over America—even in places that most people would consider unlikely, such as New England.

From quaint fishing villages on the coastlines of Maine and Rhode Island to picturesque New Hampshire towns and covered bridges, to the pastoral countryside and snow-capped mountains of Vermont, New England has long been known for its charm and beauty. But in recent years the region has become known for something else: a devastating heroin problem. In Rhode Island hospital admissions for heroin addiction rose from 5,454 in 2009 to 7,642 in 2013. Connecticut had a 48 percent increase in heroin-overdose deaths from 2012 to 2013, and heroin addiction has become such a serious problem in Massachusetts that the governor declared a public health emergency in March 2014.

> **Vermont governor Peter Shumlin is gravely concerned about his state's heroin epidemic.**

One of New England's worst heroin crises is in Vermont, where the number of people seeking treatment for heroin and other opioid abuse has risen *770 percent* since 2000. In the small town of Bennington, Vermont, where poet Robert Frost is buried behind the historic Old First Congregational Church, the heroin problem is among the worst in the state. "The quaint town of Bennington has had a rude awakening of drugs," says Vermont state trooper Wayne Godfrey, who adds that "everyone" in town is using heroin. "It's in the high school. The kids are doing it right in school. You find Baggies in the hallway."[32]

Vermont governor Peter Shumlin is gravely concerned about his state's heroin epidemic, so much so that in January 2014 he devoted his entire annual address to it. Calling the problem a "full-blown heroin crisis," Shumlin said: "In every corner of our state, heroin and opiate drug addiction threatens us. It threatens the safety that has always blessed our state. It is a crisis bubbling just beneath the surface that may be invisible to many, but is already highly visible to law enforcement, medical personnel, social service and addiction treatment providers, and too many Vermont families. It requires all of us to take action before the quality of life that we cherish so much is compromised."[33] Shumlin went on to quote a few sobering facts: Heroin overdose deaths in Vermont nearly doubled between 2012 and 2013, and the state drug task force estimates that more than $2 million of heroin and other opiates are being trafficked into Vermont every week.

New York City writer Gina Tron spent much of her childhood and adolescent years living in Vermont. She says that because people typically have such an idyllic perception of the state, they are shocked to find out that it has "such a nasty drug problem."[34] Tron has seen for herself how widespread heroin abuse is in Vermont, and she is aware of how it destroys lives. She writes:

> I can't count how many bodies of classmates and neighbors have been found in parking lots and on living room floors. In addition to the overdoses, there were also suicides—former neighbors and family friends who shot themselves to escape their addiction. And there were those who didn't get physically hurt but nonetheless destroyed their lives, like the girl who grew up down the road from me who went to federal prison before she turned 20 for heroin trafficking and illegal weapons possession. . . . It's time for Vermonters, and the rest of the country, to recognize that heroin is now nearly as much a part of our state's identity as our beloved maple syrup and covered bridges.[35]

"It's Everywhere"

Through revealing statistics, investigative findings, and innumerable first-person accounts of heroin addiction, it has become virtually impossible to ignore that the United States has a serious heroin problem. In many states, including Missouri, New Jersey, Minnesota, and the entire New England region, health officials and law enforcement professionals are grappling with the problem and trying to figure out what can be done about it. "It's penetrating our entire society," says Edward Walsh, who is police chief of Taunton, Massachusetts. "It's everywhere in our community."[36]

How Serious a Problem Is Heroin Addiction?

66 Hardly anyone will disagree that heroin is a highly addictive opiate. What's alarming is its recent resurgence as a drug of choice in America in just the past several years. 99

—Taite Adams, *Opiate Addiction: The Painkiller Addiction Epidemic, Heroin Addiction and the Way Out.* St. Petersburg, FL: Rapid Response, 2013, p. 59.

Adams (not her real name) is a former heroin addict who has been clean for more than a decade.

66 Heroin addiction, on the rise from the Pacific Northwest to the East Coast, is now claiming a new set of victims: teens and adults in the suburbs. 99

—Right Step, "Heroin: A Rising Teen Fad," January 13, 2014.

Right Step is an addiction treatment center with locations throughout Texas.

Bracketed quotes indicate conflicting positions.

* Editor's Note: While the definition of a primary source can be narrowly or broadly defined, for the purposes of Compact Research, a primary source consists of: 1) results of original research presented by an organization or researcher; 2) eyewitness accounts of events, personal experience, or work experience; 3) first-person editorials offering pundits' opinions; 4) government officials presenting political plans and/or policies; 5) representatives of organizations presenting testimony or policy.

66 Once a person becomes addicted to heroin, seeking and using the drug becomes their primary purpose in life. 99

—National Institute on Drug Abuse (NIDA), *Heroin*, Research Report Series, 2014. www.drugabuse.gov.

An agency of the National Institutes of Health, the NIDA seeks to end drug abuse and addiction in the United States.

66 Each year there are hundreds of thousands of heroin users in the United States. This number has remained stable for decades. 99

—Carl L. Hart, "Heroin (Alone) Is Not the Problem," *Huffington Post*, July 19, 2013. www.huffingtonpost.com.

Hart is a neuroscientist at Columbia University in New York City.

66 Heroin use and overdose deaths have increased in recent years. 99

—Christopher M. Jones, "Heroin Use and Heroin Use Risk Behaviors Among Nonmedical Users of Prescription Opioid Pain Relievers—United States, 2002–2004 and 2008–2010," *Drug and Alcohol Dependence*, September 2013. www.ncbi.nlm.nih.gov.

Jones, who holds a doctor of pharmacy degree and a master's in public health, is with the Centers for Disease Control and Prevention (CDC).

66 When heroin was introduced, it was believed not to be addicting. Now we know, however, that the likelihood of becoming addicted is twice as great for heroin as for morphine. 99

—Raymond Goldberg, *Drugs Across the Spectrum*. Belmont, CA: Wadsworth, 2014, p. 182.

Goldberg, who specializes in health- and drug-related topics, is dean of Health Sciences at Vance-Granville Community College in North Carolina.

66 Heroin-related overdoses and overdose deaths are increasing in certain areas, possibly due to a number of factors, such as high heroin purity, increasing numbers of heroin abusers initiating use at a younger age, and inexperienced abusers switching from prescription opioids to heroin. **99**

—US Drug Enforcement Administration (DEA), "National Drug Threat Assessment Summary," November 2013. www.justice.gov.

The DEA is the United States' leading law enforcement agency for combating the sale and distribution of narcotics and other illegal drugs.

66 Heroin use is a growing problem for law enforcement, schools, and cities. **99**

—Sherry Gaba, "Hooked on Heroin: From the Streets to the Suburbs," Good Therapy, 2013. www.goodtherapy.org.

Gaba is a family therapist from Westlake Village, California.

How Serious a Problem Is Heroin Addiction?

- According to NIDA director Nora D. Volkow, the number of people starting to use heroin has risen steadily since 2007.

- Surveys by the US Department of Health and Human Services have shown a **66 percent** increase in heroin use among Americans from 2002 to 2012, and the number of people addicted more than doubled during the same period.

- According to New York law enforcement data, heroin-related arrests on Long Island rose **163 percent** between 2013 and 2014, with the biggest increase among teenagers and young adults.

- According to the Substance Abuse and Mental Health Services Agency (SAMHSA), the greatest increase in heroin use is among young adults aged **eighteen to twenty-five.**

- After at least **185 people** in Massachusetts died of heroin overdoses between November 2013 and February 2014, the state's governor declared a public health emergency.

- According to Vermont governor Peter Shumlin, more than **$2 million** worth of heroin and other opioids are being trafficked into his state every week.

Heroin Addiction Has Soared

According to a September 2013 report by the Substance Abuse and Mental Health Services Administration (SAMHSA), the number of people in the United States with heroin dependence or abuse more than doubled from 214,000 in 2002 to 467,000 in 2012.

Number of Americans Who Were Dependent on or Used Heroin, 2002 to 2012

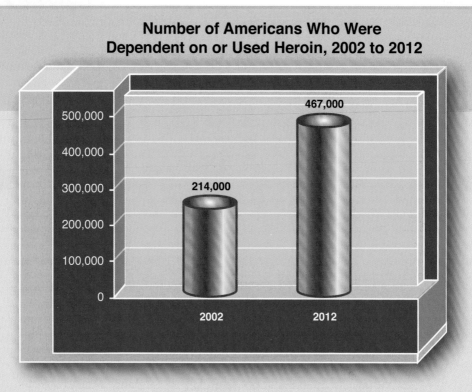

Source: Substance Abuse and Mental Health Services Administration, "Results from the 2012 National Survey on Drug Use and Health: Summary of National Findings," September 2013. www.samhsa.gov.

- The Institute for Substance Abuse Treatment Evaluation states that addicts who inject heroin typically do so up to **four times per day**.

- In 2014 US attorney general Eric Holder stated that heroin overdose deaths increased by **45 percent** between 2006 and 2010.

Rise in Heroin Addiction

Abuse of prescription painkillers is a growing problem, and studies show that a spike in heroin use and addiction in recent years is linked to abuse of these drugs. Many people become addicted to painkillers and then switch to heroin because it is cheaper and easier to get. One 2013 study found that nearly 80 percent of first-time heroin users had previously abused prescription drugs.

First-Time Heroin Users Who Did/Did Not Previously Abuse Prescription Painkillers

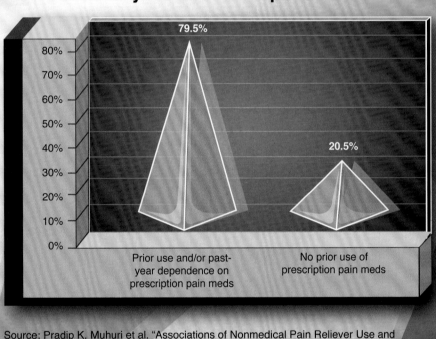

Source: Pradip K. Muhuri et al. "Associations of Nonmedical Pain Reliever Use and Initiation of Heroin Use in the United States," Substance Abuse and Mental Health Services Administration *CBHSQ Data Review*, August 2013.

- According to Mayo Clinic psychiatrist David Hall-Flavin, from 2011 to 2012 heroin overdose deaths increased by **85 percent** in Minneapolis, Minnesota.

- In 2014 the Wisconsin Department of Justice reported that the number of teens in the state between the ages of twelve and seventeen who tried heroin had increased by more than **300 percent** since 1995.

Growing Heroin Supply Contributing to Rise in Addiction

Increased availability of heroin has contributed to the worsening problem of abuse and addiction. According to the US Drug Enforcement Administration (DEA), the supply in the United States has grown steadily, largely due to increased smuggling of both Mexican- and South American–produced heroin through Mexico. This graph shows a jump in heroin seizures over a four-year period.

Heroin Seizures at the Southwest Border*—2008 Versus 2012

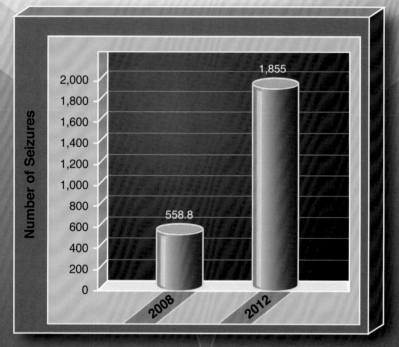

*The Southwest Border separates the United States from Mexico and stretches 1,951 miles (3,139.8 km) from San Diego, California to Brownsville, Texas.

Source: US Drug Enforcement Administration, "National Drug Threat Assessment Summary," November 2013. www.justice.gov.

- A November 2013 report by the DEA states that in Minneapolis, Minnesota, arrestees testing positive for heroin and other opiates in 2011 were much younger (nearly **20 percent** were under age twenty-one) than those testing positive for cocaine and methamphetamine.

What Are the Health Risks of Heroin Addiction?

> 66 **Heroin is an extremely dangerous drug, with a wide array of negative effects.** 99

—Nora D. Volkow, director of the National Institute on Drug Abuse.

> 66 **In a short amount of time, regular heroin use destroys the body.** 99

—Above the Influence, an antidrug organization affiliated with Partnership for Drug-Free Kids.

Brian Rinker started using heroin when he was twenty-one years old, and he was addicted to the drug for the next five years. Now a journalist living in San Francisco, California, Rinker has written numerous articles about his time as an addict, and he has spoken freely about how heroin affected his life and his health. "In the depths of my addiction," he says, "I've risked death and disease."[37] Among Rinker's worst problems were abscesses, which are pus-filled infections also known as boils. In intravenous drug users, abscesses are usually caused by infectious bacteria from dirty needles or dirt and grime on the skin. The bacteria get into the bloodstream after being pushed through the skin by the puncture of the needle. The bacteria multiply, leading to inflammation and the formation of a swollen, pus-filled mass.

Rinker refers to abscesses as "nasty and dangerous."[38] He says they are common among junkies, and when he was using heroin he used to get them all the time. One abscess in particular stands out vividly in his mind because it was so massive and painful—and the infection nearly caused him to lose his leg.

Excruciating Pain

Abscesses formed inside Rinker's muscle tissue because of the way he injected heroin. As is common among drug addicts who have shot up repeatedly over a long period of time, his veins had either collapsed or hardened. So, in the absence of accessible veins, he used a technique called "muscling," whereby he injected heroin deep into the muscles of his shoulders, thighs, and buttocks. This ultimately led to intramuscular abscesses, such as one in his left thigh that was worse than any he had ever had before.

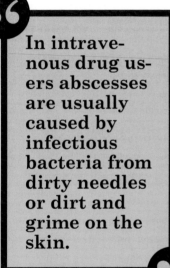

In intravenous drug users abscesses are usually caused by infectious bacteria from dirty needles or dirt and grime on the skin.

For quite a while after the abscess formed Rinker put off seeking medical attention. "I had waited until the last minute before finally going to the emergency room," he says. "For weeks, I hobbled around on a cane, hoping the abscess would just go away." The abscess did not "just go away." The infection continued to worsen until Rinker's thigh had swollen to nearly twice its normal size. "The pain was so intense that I would wake up in the middle of the night in agony, my thigh throbbing," he says. "It was unbearable."[39]

At the emergency room the doctor said that Rinker needed surgery. Rinker tried to object, but the doctor warned that he could lose his leg or die, so he reluctantly agreed. When he regained consciousness after the operation, the surgeon gave him the good news that his leg was saved. But because the abscess had grown so big, some major cutting was necessary to remove it. "I had a hole in my left thigh the size of two grapefruits,"[40] says Rinker.

Life-Threatening Liver Disease

Abscesses are only one example of the health problems posed by heroin abuse; whenever addicts use the drug, they are putting their health at serious risk. "No matter how they ingest the drug," says the NIDA, "chronic heroin users experience a variety of medical complications."[41] The agency cites many different risks of heroin abuse, from lung complications to mental disorders such as depression and antisocial personality disorder. The NIDA also says that the sharing of needles among intravenous drug users can lead to some of the "most severe consequences of heroin abuse."[42] This is in reference to users becoming infected with HIV, the virus that causes AIDS; or the hepatitis B and C viruses, which cause the diseases hepatitis B and hepatitis C. All types of hepatitis are infectious diseases of the liver. Without treatment they can lead to chronic (long-term) liver disease or cancer of the liver.

As the incidence of heroin addiction has steadily grown in the United States, health officials have observed an alarming trend: a corresponding rise in the incidence of hepatitis C. In a 2013 report by the US Department of Health and Human Services this trend is referred to as an "emerging epidemic" and "a serious health concern."[43] This spike in hepatitis C cases was found to be most prevalent among young intravenous drug users, both male and female, usually Caucasian, from regions throughout the United States but primarily in suburban and rural areas. Since 2007, the report states, deaths in the United States associated with hepatitis C have surpassed deaths associated with HIV.

> " As the incidence of heroin addiction has steadily grown in the United States, health officials have observed an alarming trend: a corresponding rise in the incidence of hepatitis C. "

The increase in hepatitis C among young people was first discovered and reported by the Massachusetts Department of Public Health. After noticing a mysterious jump in the number of cases, the agency analyzed infection data and found that between 2002 and 2009 there was a significant increase of hepatitis C among teens and young adults aged fifteen to twenty-four. In-depth interviews with the affected individuals revealed that most were intravenous drug users who became addicted to heroin after abusing prescription opioids. Further investigations showed that health departments in regions across the country were observing similar findings. The concern of health officials over this nationwide spike of hepatitis C was explained in a May 2011 report by the Centers for Disease Control and Prevention (CDC): "The recent epidemic in reported cases among adolescents and young adults and its apparent association with increases in drug injection and sharing of injection equipment in this population is a disturbing trend."[44]

Brain Changes

Scientists have long known that when someone uses heroin, it changes back into morphine and then binds to opioid receptors in the brain. This is what causes the notorious euphoric rush, and also what keeps addicts returning to the drug again and again. That high is seductive—and to a hard-core heroin addict, impossible to resist. "Regular heroin use changes the functioning of the brain," says the NIDA. "One result is tolerance, in which more of the drug is needed to achieve the same intensity of effect. Another result is dependence, characterized by the need to continue use of the drug to avoid withdrawal symptoms."[45]

Despite all that is known about heroin addiction, many questions remain unanswered. For example, what are the long-term effects on brain function of repeated heroin use? At least part of the answer may be found in a study published in November 2013. The study was led by Yasmin Hurd, a psychiatry professor at the Icahn School of Medicine at Mount Sinai Hospital in New York City. Hurd and her colleagues studied the brains of heroin addicts who had died, with a particular focus on an area of the brain called the striatum, which plays a key role in addiction. The researchers found marked changes in how DNA had been used in the brains, and the level of change was closely related to how long the individuals had remained addicted. The study ultimately revealed that long-term heroin abuse alters how genes are activated in the brain, which can alter how it functions. "Our study addresses a critical gap in our knowledge about heroin addiction," says Hurd, "because we cannot often directly

> **That high is seductive—and to a hard-core heroin addict, impossible to resist.**

study the brains of addicted humans. Our results provide important insights into how human brains change in response to long-term heroin use, and give us knowledge to help treat this dangerous disease."[46]

Pregnant and Addicted

A pregnant woman who uses heroin is risking damage not only to herself but also to her unborn child. Some of the problems heroin use during pregnancy can cause include spontaneous abortion (miscarriage); stillbirth, meaning the baby dies in the womb before birth but after twenty weeks of pregnancy; premature birth; low birth weight; and birth defects. Heroin abuse during pregnancy can also cause a serious condition known as placental abruption, which the March of Dimes says can cause very heavy bleeding "and can be deadly for both mother and baby."[47]

Another problem associated with women who use heroin during pregnancy is a condition known as neonatal abstinence syndrome, or neonatal withdrawal syndrome. This is when heroin used by the mother passes through the placenta to the fetus during pregnancy. Thus, when the baby is born, he or she is addicted just as the mother is. The University of Rochester Medical Center explains: "Almost every drug passes from the mother's blood stream through the placenta to the fetus. Illicit substances that cause drug dependence and addiction in the mother also cause the fetus to become addicted. At birth, the baby's dependence on the substance continues. However, since the drug is no longer available, the baby's central nervous system becomes overstimulated causing the symptoms of withdrawal."[48] The group goes on to say that some drugs are more likely to cause neonatal abstinence syndrome than others. More than half of all babies exposed to opioids such as heroin prenatally will suffer from the condition. It can result in severe withdrawal symptoms that cause the baby such distress he or she often must be hospitalized. In some cases neonatal abstinence syndrome can be fatal.

Overdose Dangers

People often have the impression that when someone dies of a heroin overdose the death was caused by the person taking too much of the drug, but that is only partially true. Experts say that most people who overdose die because they lose consciousness and "forget to breathe." Karen Drexler, who is an associate professor in Emory University's psychiatry and behavioral sciences department, explains: "Heroin makes someone calm and a little bit sleepy, but if you take too much then you can fall asleep, and when you are asleep your respiratory drive shuts down." Drexler adds that under normal conditions when people are asleep their bodies naturally remember to breathe. "In the case of a heroin overdose," she says, "you fall asleep and essentially your body forgets."[49]

> **People often have the impression that when someone dies of a heroin overdose the death was caused by the person taking too much of the drug, but that is not necessarily true.**

Although there is no way for health officials to determine exact numbers, not everyone who overdoses on heroin dies. If someone who has injected the drug starts exhibiting symptoms such as shallow breathing, low blood pressure, weak pulse, bluish-colored nails and lips, and extremely small pupils (known as "pinpoint pupils"), the person has likely overdosed and can be saved if he or she receives immediate medical attention. Paramedics throughout the country carry an emergency antidote medication known as naloxone, which can counter the effects of an overdose of heroin or other opioids. "In many cases," says Rinker, "there is no reason a person should die from an overdose, especially from opiates." He adds that naloxone is sometimes given out at needle exchanges in the form of a take-home nasal spray. "It's worked miracles," says Rinker. "Before the widespread use of naloxone, hundreds died every year from heroin-related overdoses in [San Francisco]. From 2010 to early 2012, just eight died."[50]

Rinker is personally familiar with a heroin overdose because he came close to dying from one during his years as an addict. He says it was early in his "junkie career," and he did not yet know how much heroin was safe to inject. He was having trouble finding a vein, so his friend put the needle in his arm for him. The effects of the drug were immediate. "A hot wave rushed through me," says Rinker. "Nausea. I was so tired. The world closed in. I slid off the couch and everything went black." The next thing he noticed was the light slowly fading back in so he could see again. He did not know until later that his eyes had been wide open the whole time, which terrified his friend. "He seemed frantic—almost foolish," says Rinker. "I couldn't hear anything, but I could see his silent screams. I had overdosed. My friend said I turned blue and gurgled. . . . He sat on my chest and tried to slap me awake. He was afraid to call 911."[51] Rinker recovered from the overdose, but he is fully aware that he came perilously close to dying.

Infinite Dangers

Using SAMHSA's estimates, nearly five hundred thousand people in the United States are addicted to heroin, with countless others using the drug on occasion—and every one of those users is risking health problems and perhaps death. From intramuscular abscesses to chronic liver disease, and from changes in brain function to the possibility of overdose, the list of ways heroin users can harm themselves is virtually endless.

What Are the Health Risks of Heroin Addiction?

❝In addition to the effects of the drug itself, street heroin often contains toxic contaminants or additives that can clog blood vessels leading to the lungs, liver, kidneys, or brain, causing permanent damage to vital organs.❞

—National Institute on Drug Abuse (NIDA), "Heroin," *Drug Facts*, April 2013. www.drugabuse.gov.

An agency of the National Institutes of Health, the NIDA seeks to end drug abuse and addiction in the United States.

❝It is not uncommon for heroin addicts to commit suicide.❞

—Raymond Goldberg, *Drugs Across the Spectrum*. Belmont, CA: Wadsworth, 2014, p. 186.

Goldberg, who specializes in health- and drug-related topics, is dean of Health Sciences at Vance-Granville Community College in North Carolina.

Bracketed quotes indicate conflicting positions.

* Editor's Note: While the definition of a primary source can be narrowly or broadly defined, for the purposes of Compact Research, a primary source consists of: 1) results of original research presented by an organization or researcher; 2) eyewitness accounts of events, personal experience, or work experience; 3) first-person editorials offering pundits' opinions; 4) government officials presenting political plans and/or policies; 5) representatives of organizations presenting testimony or policy.

❝Certainly, we've seen the gut-wrenching portrayals of heroin addicts agonizing, especially when experiencing withdrawal from the drug.❞

—Carl L. Hart, "Heroin (Alone) Is Not the Problem," *Huffington Post*, July 19, 2013. www.huffingtonpost.com.

Hart is a neuroscientist at Columbia University in New York City.

❝A heroin overdose can result in seizures, a coma, or even death.❞

—Sherry Gaba, "Hooked on Heroin: From the Streets to the Suburbs," Good Therapy, 2013. www.goodtherapy.org.

Gaba is a family therapist from Westlake Village, California.

❝Besides the physical dangers associated with heroin addiction, there are many psychological and relational ones as well. Individuals hooked on heroin may become depressed, psychotic, and paranoid.❞

—Taite Adams, *Opiate Addiction: The Painkiller Addiction Epidemic, Heroin Addiction and the Way Out.* St. Petersburg, FL: Rapid Response, 2013, p. 66.

Adams (not her real name) is a former heroin addict who has been clean for more than a decade.

❝Those abusers who have recently switched to heroin are at higher risk for accidental overdose.❞

—US Drug Enforcement Administration (DEA), "National Drug Threat Assessment Summary," November 2013. www.justice.gov.

The DEA is the United States' leading law enforcement agency for combating the sale and distribution of narcotics and other illegal drugs.

66 One truism of addiction science is that long-term abuse rewires your brain and changes its chemistry . . . but these changes can be reversed over time. **99**

—Seth Mnookin, "Why Philip Seymour Hoffman's Death Is So Scary," *Slate*, February 4, 2014. www.slate.com.

A recovering heroin addict, Mnookin is now associate director of the science writing program at the Massachusetts Institute of Technology (MIT).

66 Because of the many places opiates can work in the brain, they are particularly menacing. **99**

—Timothy P. Condon, "Hoffman's Death Illustrates Heroin's Ability to Hijack the Brain," *Huffington Post*, April 15, 2014. www.huffingtonpost.com.

Condon is chief science adviser to the Center for Health and Justice.

Facts and Illustrations

What Are the Health Risks of Heroin Addiction?

- According to the World Health Organization, regular heroin users have a **twenty to thirty times** higher risk of accidental death than nonusers.

- A February 2012 report by the director of Missouri's Department of Health and Senior Services states that the incidence of major depression is extremely high among heroin users, and the risk of suicide is **fourteen times greater** than that of the general population.

- According to the Centers for Disease Control and Prevention, US drug poisoning deaths involving heroin increased by **45 percent** from 2006 to 2010.

- An April 2014 report by the NIDA shows that of the seventeen thousand new Hepatitis C infections in the United States during 2010, **more than half** were among people who used drugs by injection.

- Medical research has shown that intravenous heroin users have a high risk of developing a life-threatening heart condition known as infective endocarditis.

- According to the addiction recovery organization Narconon, heroin reduces the action of muscles in the intestines, making constipation a constant problem.

Heroin Is Hazardous to Health

People who habitually use heroin can do serious harm to their bodies, from developing skin infections to contracting liver, heart, and kidney disease. Overdose is also a serious risk.

Short-Term Effects of Heroin Use	Long-Term Effects of Heroin Use
Clouded mental functioning (following initial rush)	Abscesses (pus-filled infections)
Dry mouth	Collapsed veins
Heavy feeling in arms and legs	Infection of the heart lining and valves
Nausea and vomiting	Liver disease
Severe itching	Lung-related complications such as pneumonia
Respiratory failure due to dramatic slowdown in breathing (the cause of most overdose deaths)	Life-threatening clogging of blood vessels in lungs, liver, kidneys, or brain, caused by additives in herion that do not easily dilute in the bloodstream
	HIV (virus that causes AIDS), hepatitis B, and hepatitis C from using contaminated needles
	Death from respiratory failure

Source: University of Maryland Center for Substance Abuse Research, "Heroin," October 29, 2013. www.cesar.umd.edu.

- The Maryland Department of Health and Mental Hygiene released a report in 2014 showing that the number of heroin-related overdose deaths increased **54 percent** between 2011 and 2012.

- According to a February 2014 report by the NIDA, each intravenous heroin user who contracts a liver disease known as hepatitis C is likely to infect **twenty other people**.

- A February 2012 report by the director of Missouri's Department of Health and Senior Services states that **99 percent** of overdose deaths from heroin occur among users who injected it.

Nationwide Spike in Overdose Deaths

Addiction experts emphasize that every time people use heroin, especially if they inject it, dying from an overdose is a very real risk. According to an Associated Press investigation released in April 2014, states throughout America have seen an alarming increase in heroin-related deaths.

State	Heroin-Related Overdose Deaths
Colorado	6 teens died in the past 12 years, compared with 5 teens who died in 2012 alone.
Connecticut	In 2012 deaths totaled 174 and jumped to 257 in 2013—a 48 percent increase.
Florida	Deaths nearly doubled between 2011 and 2012, from 57 to 108.
Illinois	In DuPage County deaths stayed in the 20s from 2007 to 2011, then rose to 43 in 2012 and 46 in 2013; in Madison County deaths totaled 23 in 2013, up from 7 deaths in 2009.
Louisiana	Deaths rose from 5 in 2008 to 110 in 2012.
Massachusetts	185 people died between November 2013 and April 2014, not including heroin-related deaths in the state's largest cities. Opiate overdose deaths (heroin and/or prescription pain meds) totaled 642 in 2011, nearly double the number from 2000.
Michigan	Increase in deaths from 271 in 2002 to 728 in 2012.
Minnesota	Deaths jumped from 3 in 1999 to 50 in 2011, 49 in 2012, and (according to preliminary data) 98 in 2013.
Missouri	State records from 2001 show 18 deaths, compared with 245 in 2011.
New Hampshire	2008 deaths totaled 16, jumping to 38 in 2012 and 68 in 2013.
New Jersey	In 2012, 591 people died, up from 443 in 2011.
North Carolina	Deaths averaged between 40 and 50 during the 2000s then spiked to 77 in 2011 and 148 in 2012.
Ohio	In 2010 deaths totaled 338 and increased to 426 in 2011.
Oregon	Several dozen deaths were reported each year from 2000 to 2008 and then started averaging more than 100 per year.
Texas	During the period of 1999 to 2011, deaths jumped from 111 to 364.
Vermont	After remaining in the single digits for years, deaths totaled 21 in 2013.
Virginia	Deaths have steadily increased since 2011 when the total was 101, rising to 135 in 2012 and 197 in 2013.
Washington	Deaths have soared from 16 in 1995 to 182 in 2012.
West Virginia	In 2007 deaths totaled 22 and by 2012 (preliminary data) had risen to 70.

Source: Andrew Welsh-Huggins, "The Big Story: A Look at Heroin Use, Deaths in Some US States," AP, April 5, 2014. http://bigstory.ap.org.

- According to the Partnership at Drugfree.org, sudden withdrawal from heroin by heavily dependent users in poor health can be fatal.

- A June 2013 report by Washington State's Alcohol and Drug Abuse Institute reveals that in King County, Washington, **75 percent** of injection drug users suffer from hepatitis C.

- According to the March of Dimes, babies born to mothers who are addicted to heroin are at greater risk of SIDS (sudden infant death syndrome).

- A February 2014 NBC News report revealed that between September 2013 and January 2014, **thirty-seven people** died after using heroin that had been tainted with a powerful synthetic opioid known as fentanyl.

Can People Overcome Heroin Addiction?

“There is a way out from heroin addiction and those who have found it will gladly tell you that it is much easier than the pains and fears that come with the day to day life of an IV drug addict.”

—Taite Adams (not her real name), a former heroin addict and the author of *Opiate Addiction: The Painkiller Addiction Epidemic, Heroin Addiction and the Way Out.*

“Most alcoholics and addicts don’t stay sober.”

—Brian Rinker, a former heroin addict who is now a journalist living in San Francisco.

On the evening of February 5, 2014, the blazing lights of New York City’s Broadway theater district faded to darkness and stayed that way for one full minute. This was not caused by a power outage; rather, the theaters collectively dimmed their lights to honor the memory of one of their own, the acclaimed stage and screen actor Philip Seymour Hoffman. Three days before, the forty-six-year-old Hoffman had been found dead in his Manhattan apartment with a needle still in his forearm. Investigators discovered more than sixty bags of heroin in the apartment as well as empty heroin bags and used syringes.

Hoffman’s family and friends were devastated by his death. His innumerable fans also mourned him, and many were shocked that he would die of an overdose. Even though Hoffman had talked freely about his difficult battle with heroin addiction, he had stopped using drugs while in his twenties and remained clean and sober for twenty-three years. Addiction experts emphasize, however, that relapse is always a danger for an addict no matter how long he or she has been sober—even if decades have passed. "We treat addiction like you can make it go away with a 28-day stint in rehab and that's the end of it, but that's not how it works," says psychiatrist Joseph A. Shrand, who is medical director of a teen addiction treatment center in Brockton, Massachusetts. "It requires lifelong vigilance to stay clean."[52]

The Grim Reality of Relapse

The likelihood of relapse is one of the most disturbing aspects of heroin addiction; research has shown that up to 90 percent of addicts return to using drugs. According to Shrand, relapses are common because drug addiction is a chronic condition not that different from diabetes or heart disease. In the same way that those diseases cannot be cured and must be managed throughout a person's lifetime, the same is true of addiction. So the risk of relapse is high even for someone like Hoffman who was drug-free for many years. In fact, long-term sober addicts are especially at risk because as time passes they can develop a false sense of security. "They get it in their mind that they can go back to using just once or just a little," says Shrand. "Or maybe they think that they can use another substance other than their substance of choice and be fine, but they can't. It just takes one moment of weakness to lead them down a path of destruction."[53]

> On the evening of February 5, 2014, the blazing lights of New York City's Broadway theater district faded to darkness and stayed that way for one full minute.

During a June 2006 interview on the television program *60 Minutes*, Hoffman talked candidly about his past as an alcohol and drug addict, saying he took anything he could get his hands on. When asked about his current abstinence from drugs and alcohol, Hoffman confirmed that he had been clean and sober since being in rehab when he was twenty-two years old. When asked why he stopped using, he replied, "I got panicked for my life."[54] In 2012, after more than two decades of sobriety, Hoffman relapsed and checked into a detox facility. Less than a year later he was found dead in his apartment by a close friend.

Detox and Beyond

Although relapse is common among heroin addicts, it is not inevitable. Many addicts are able to stay clean after treatment and go on to live drug-free lives. But overcoming heroin addiction takes a great deal of motivation, commitment, and willingness to work hard and to do whatever is needed to get better. The process starts with detox, which refers to abstinence from drugs while the addict's bloodstream is cleansed of all traces of toxins. Because heroin addicts suffer from severe withdrawal during detox, addiction experts stress the importance of medical supervision. Many experts also recommend that addicts be given prescription drugs that can help ease their suffering and improve their chances of success. The NIDA explains: "Scientific research has established that medication-assisted treatment of opioid addiction increases patient retention and decreases drug use."[55]

> " The likelihood of relapse is one of the most disturbing aspects of heroin addiction; research has shown that up to 90 percent of addicts return to using drugs. "

The NIDA goes on to explain that medications such as methadone, buprenorphine, and naltrexone can play an important role in this phase of the patient's recovery. "Acting on the same targets in the brain as heroin and morphine," says the NIDA, "methadone and buprenorphine suppress withdrawal symptoms and relieve cravings. Naltrexone works by blocking the effects of heroin or other opioids at their receptor sites and should only be used in patients who have already been detoxified. . . . All medications help patients disengage from drug seeking and related criminal behavior and become more receptive to behavioral treatments."[56]

Addiction experts stress that once detoxification is complete, it is important for the patient to continue with treatment by participating

> **Because heroin addicts suffer from severe withdrawal during detox, addiction experts stress the importance of medical supervision.**

in one or more form of psychotherapy, such as individual, group, and/or family. He or she may attend therapy sessions on an outpatient basis or stay at a residential treatment center, the latter of which offers the greatest advantages to addiction patients. At residential facilities the patient receives intensive psychotherapy, often several different types, and is monitored around the clock. "We do often recommend that heroin addicts stay in treatment for at least 60 days," says psychiatrist Barbara Krantz, who is medical director of the Hanley Center drug rehabilitation facility in West Palm Beach, Florida. "We find that individuals addicted to heroin need extensive time in treatment because of how much the drug impacts their brain and behavior. Cravings can be intense and they need to relearn how to deal with life stressors and be able to use non-chemical coping skills."[57]

A Healing Place for Teens

A long-term residential treatment facility that has a record of success with young heroin addicts is called Outreach House. Located in Long Island, New York, the facility serves adolescents aged twelve to seventeen. For the teens who are treated at Outreach House the days are packed with activities including a full day of school; different kinds of psychotherapy, such as individual, group, vocational, and family; and a variety of health and recreational programs that are designed to strengthen the body and mind. No distractions to recovery are allowed at the facility; patients cannot have cell phones or personal televisions, nor can they use computers for purposes other than doing homework. All teens hold mandatory jobs, such as being part of a service crew, and all are given opportunities to work up to leadership positions. Supervisors emphasize the importance of young people taking responsibility for their own behavior.

One heroin addict who was able to recover with the help of Outreach House is a Long Island teenager named Chris. During the height of his addiction Chris was spending hundreds of dollars a day on heroin. "I was stealing money from my parents," he says, "I was doing illegal actions with my friends, I broke into houses, I've done all of the above besides selling myself."[58] Chris tried short-term treatment programs three different times but all he gained was new connections with other addicts; after each program ended, he put those connections to work and went right back to using.

When Chris entered Outreach House, the idea of being there for nearly a year was overwhelming—so much so that he ran away five times in the first few months. But eventually he stayed at Outreach, worked hard toward overcoming his addiction, and began to make progress. The days and months passed and by the time Chris had spent eleven months at the facility, he was ready to graduate. He credits the program with saving his life, as he explains: "I put myself in so many circumstances where I could have died. Being able to say that I have different ways that I can manage my emotions besides getting high, it makes me very happy and excited to go through my future."[59]

Hurdles to Treatment

Few addiction specialists would disagree that long-term residential treatment programs are the ideal solution for heroin addicts. Studies have shown that these facilities often succeed where others have failed. A major problem, however, is that such facilities are in short supply in the United States. According to data compiled by the Treatment Research Institute in Philadelphia, Pennsylvania, there are about twelve thousand addiction treatment programs nationwide. Of those only 10 percent are residential facilities, about 80 percent are outpatient programs, and 10 percent are drug treatment clinics. "There's not enough beds, there's not enough providers," says health educator Bruno Silie, who helps place addicts in treatment facilities in Atlantic City, New Jersey. "There's options, but the waiting period is ridiculous. I've had clients wait for 60-plus days, and by that time they've given up."[60]

One of the biggest challenges for heroin addicts who are motivated to get better is that treatment can be terribly expensive—especially long-term residential programs. According to the Minnesota-based treatment provider Hazelden, the cost of a stay at a residential alcohol and drug rehabilitation facility ranges from $20,000 to $32,000 depending on the level of services needed. An April 7, 2014, article in the publication *Busi-*

ness Insider says that the average cost of an inpatient facility is $30,000—for thirty days. Treatment facilities where patients reside for six months to a year are far more expensive, meaning they are out of reach for the average family. Health insurance plans typically cover some of the cost of treatment but often have a limit on the number of months (or days) for which they will pay. Because of these limitations, the Association for Addiction Professionals (NAADAC) estimates that only about 10 percent of Americans who are addicted to heroin or other opioids receive any sort of treatment.

Mentoring in Oregon

It is widely believed that no one understands addiction quite like a recovering addict, which is one reason why David Fitzgerald's program is working so well. Fitzgerald founded and directs the mentoring program at Central City Concern, one of the best known and most successful drug rehabilitation clinics in Portland, Oregon. He joined Central City after a rocky background that included more than twenty years in prison. Like so many incarcerated addicts even Fitzgerald's time behind bars was spent addicted to drugs, and he says that heroin was the worst of them all. In 1997 Fitzgerald finally got sober, and he joined Central City Concern two years later.

> " Although people can and do overcome heroin addiction, there are numerous hurdles for those who seek treatment. "

From the very beginning Fitzgerald could tell that Central City's way of treating addiction was not effective. Addicts who were admitted to the clinic spent seven or eight days being detoxed and were then handed a list of tasks to be completed independently. They were directed to find work, meet with their probation officer, and locate the site where their daily box of food would be dropped off. "Like they're going to do any of that," Fitzgerald scoffs. The reality, he says, is that once they finish detox the "first thing they do is see somebody they know, get that fix."[61] Fitzgerald revamped the program to focus on mentoring, with recovered addicts keeping close tabs on those who are still struggling and vulnerable. Mentors accompany clients to look for permanent housing, ensure that their daytime hours are filled with tasks, and require that clients spend their free time at the clinic, which is also where they sleep at night until they are able to live independently.

With a 60 percent success rate, Central City Concern is known as one of the most successful addiction treatment facilities. During his years with the facility Fitzgerald has seen people succeed at overcoming their addiction, as well as others who do not make it—and some who have lost their lives because of addiction. He is realistic enough to know that many of his current clients will relapse and come back for help again. He hopes, though, that what they learn from his program and their mentors will make a positive difference in their lives. "That's about all you can do," he says, "hope some of it sticks."[62]

Tough to Overcome

Although people can and do overcome heroin addiction, there are numerous hurdles for those who seek treatment. The best option for recovery is a residential treatment center, but the demand for such programs far exceeds their availability. The facilities that do exist are often much too expensive for most people to afford. Programs such as Outreach House are successful because they use a mentoring approach, but those are also in short supply. And one of the biggest challenges is that no matter how many years have gone by, addicts are always at risk for relapse.

Can People Overcome Heroin Addiction?

❝One reason for addicts not seeking treatment is the fear of withdrawal, characterized by insomnia, diarrhea, irritability, and aches and pains. Addicts are not likely to die during withdrawal, though.❞

—Raymond Goldberg, *Drugs Across the Spectrum*. Belmont, CA: Wadsworth, 2014, p. 190.

Goldberg, who specializes in health- and drug-related topics, is dean of Health Sciences at Vance-Granville Community College in North Carolina.

❝A range of treatments including behavioral therapies and medications are effective at helping patients stop using heroin and return to stable and productive lives.❞

—National Institute on Drug Abuse (NIDA), "Heroin," *Drug Facts*, April 2013. www.drugabuse.gov.

An agency of the National Institutes of Health, the NIDA seeks to end drug abuse and addiction in the United States.

Bracketed quotes indicate conflicting positions.

* Editor's Note: While the definition of a primary source can be narrowly or broadly defined, for the purposes of Compact Research, a primary source consists of: 1) results of original research presented by an organization or researcher; 2) eyewitness accounts of events, personal experience, or work experience; 3) first-person editorials offering pundits' opinions; 4) government officials presenting political plans and/or policies; 5) representatives of organizations presenting testimony or policy.

“We find that individuals addicted to heroin need extensive time in treatment because of how the drug impacts their brain and behavior.”

—Barbara Krantz, “Commentary: What You Need to Know About Heroin Addiction,” Partnership at Drugfree.org, February 12, 2014. www.drugfree.org.

Krantz is medical director at the Hanley Center, a drug and alcohol rehabilitation facility in West Palm Beach, Florida.

‥‥‥

“For most people, relapse is not the end of recovery; it’s another step on the journey.”

—David Sack, “When Relapse Turns Deadly: What You Need to Know About Drug Overdose,” *Huffington Post*, July 22, 2013. www.huffingtonpost.com.

Sack is board certified in psychiatry, addiction psychiatry, and addiction medicine, and is CEO of Elements Behavioral Health.

‥‥‥

“Some rehabs—and some insurance companies—perpetuate the myth that people who make it through detox are fully treated and are ready to rebuild their lives.”

—David Sheff, *Clean: Overcoming Addiction and Ending America’s Greatest Tragedy*. New York: Houghton Mifflin Harcourt, 2013, p. 144.

Sheff is a journalist and author whose son, Nic, has battled addiction to numerous drugs, including heroin and crystal meth.

‥‥‥

“Medications are available to treat heroin addiction while reducing drug cravings and withdrawal symptoms, improving the odds of achieving abstinence.”

—Nora D. Volkow, *Heroin*, “Director’s Page,” Research Report Series, National Institute on Drug Abuse, April 2014. www.drugabuse.gov.

Volkow is director of the National Institute on Drug Abuse.

‥‥‥

❝The lifetime commitment to abstinence from drugs is what kills many people. When they have cravings to use, the stigma attached to heroin use forces them to deal or not deal with their affliction in private.❞

—Tracey Helton Mitchell, "I Went from Heroin Addict to PTA Mom," CNN, February 4, 2014. www.cnn.com.

Mitchell is a woman from San Francisco who overcame an eight-year addiction to heroin.

❝We do know that relapse rates for drug and alcohol addiction are comparable to people's inability to control other chronic illnesses, such as type 2 diabetes, asthma, and hypertension.❞

—Seth Mnookin, "Why Philip Seymour Hoffman's Death Is So Scary," *Slate*, February 4, 2014. www.slate.com.

A recovering heroin addict, Mnookin is now associate director of the science writing program at the Massachusetts Institute of Technology (MIT).

❝Terrific advances in treatment have been achieved, but this progress must race ahead of the wave of opiate addiction that is crossing the country.❞

—Timothy P. Condon, "Hoffman's Death Illustrates Heroin's Ability to Hijack the Brain," *Huffington Post*, April 15, 2014. www.huffingtonpost.com.

Condon is chief science adviser to the Center for Health and Justice.

Facts and Illustrations

Can People Overcome Heroin Addiction?

- A January 2014 NIDA fact sheet states that in 2012 an estimated **23 million** Americans needed treatment for a problem related to drugs or alcohol, but only about **10 percent** received treatment at a specialized facility.

- A 2013 report by SAMHSA states that of the **1.1 million** Americans aged twelve or older who felt they needed help for a drug or alcohol problem, about **31 percent** made an effort to get treatment.

- According to Scott Krakower, who is assistant unit chief of psychiatry at Zucker Hillside Hospital in Queens, New York, users of opioid drugs such as heroin have a relapse rate as high as **80 percent**, which is much higher than for users of other types of drugs.

- A 2014 investigation by the Associated Press found that admissions for heroin addiction in Rhode Island rose **41 percent** in 2013 with the highest growth among the thirty-one- to forty-five-year-old group.

- According to the addiction treatment organization Michael's House, about **14 percent** of people entering treatment for drug addiction cite heroin as their drug of choice.

Easing the Pain of Withdrawal

Heroin addiction is very difficult to overcome, but recovery is possible if addicts are motivated to get clean and willing to work hard to make that happen. Although treatment plans differ based on the needs of the patient, many addiction specialists and treatment providers recommend medications such as those shown here.

Drug	What It Is	What It Does	Additional Information
Methadone	A synthetic opioid that has been the standard form of medication-assisted treatment for heroin addiction for more than 30 years.	When used properly, methadone suppresses withdrawal symptoms and reduces cravings. Also, participation in a methadone program has been shown to improve both physical and mental health, and decrease heroin-related deaths	Disadvantage: methadone is only available from federally regulated clinics, which are few in number and unappealing to most patients.
Naltrexone	An opioid blocker designed to treat addiction to heroin and other opioids but which cannot be started until the patient has been detoxed and off all opioids for at least two weeks.	If the patient uses heroin or other opioids during naltrexone treatment, it blocks the euphoric and pain-relieving effects of those drugs.	Disadvantage: naltrexone does not suppress withdrawal or cravings; also, once patients have started on it the risk of overdose is increased if they relapse and use opioids.
Buprenorphine	A semi-synthetic opioid that, unlike methadone, can be prescribed by a physician rather than being limited to federally regulated clinics.	Suppresses withdrawal symptoms and cravings for heroin and other opioids; does not cause euphoria in opioid-dependent patients; and blocks the effects of the problem opioids for at least 24 hours.	Studies have shown success rates for buprenorphine treatment to be as high as 40 to 60 percent; and because it does not cause euphoria in patients with opioid addiction, its abuse potential is low.

Source: Jeffrey Stockers, "How Is Suboxone Treatment Different than Drug Abuse?," Psych Central, January 30, 2013. http://psychcentral.com.

- Margaret T. Donnelly, director of Missouri's Department of Health and Senior Services, states that enrollment in treatment has proved to substantially reduce the risk of both fatal and nonfatal heroin overdose.

- A 2014 investigation by Associated Press found that admissions to publicly funded programs for heroin treatment in Michigan nearly doubled, from **7,300** in 2000 to **13,600** in 2013.

The Treatment Gap

Although treatment can help people recover from heroin addiction and go on to live healthy, drug-free lives, most of those who need to be treated never are. As this graph shows in 2012 less than 11 percent of drug addicts (heroin and other illicit drugs) and alcoholics were treated at a specialized facility, meaning one that specializes in alcohol or drug addiction.

Illicit Drug or Alcohol Abuse: Treatment Needed Versus Treatment Received, 2012

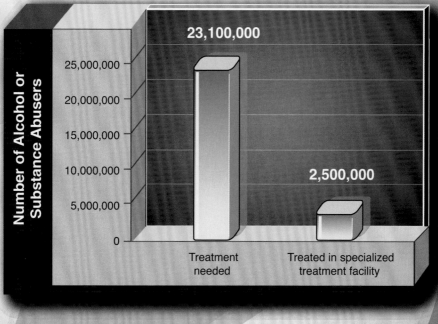

Source: Substance Abuse and Mental Health Services Administration, "Substance Use Trends in 2012," *SAMHSA News*, Fall 2013.

- According to the NIDA, scientific research has established that the use of medications to treat heroin and other opioid addiction increases retention in treatment programs and decreases drug use, infectious disease transmission, and criminal activity.

- According to the addiction recovery organization Narconon, only a small number of heroin addicts request help because most fear the pain and sickness of withdrawal.

- A 2014 investigation by the Associated Press found that admission to treatment programs for heroin addiction in Missouri rose **700 percent** over the past twenty years.

- The addiction recovery organization Narconon says that it has a **70 percent** success rate at helping heroin addicts recover.

What Can Be Done About Heroin Addiction?

66We wring our hands about overdoses, but do little to make effective treatment widely available. Our continuing refusal to prevent and treat addiction is a medical and social scandal.99

—David Rosenbloom, professor of health policy and management at Boston University's School of Public Health and Boston's former commissioner of health and hospitals.

66The heroin epidemic is dangerous, startling, and tragic. But it is far from hopeless. The solutions are in front of us, and research continues to provide more answers every day.99

—Timothy P. Condon, chief science adviser to the Center for Health and Justice.

With the incidence of heroin abuse growing at an alarming pace and overdose deaths continuing to climb, US law enforcement officials, health care providers, addiction experts, and advocacy groups are seeking answers to how this disturbing trend can be stopped. Since the early 1970s and the start of the war on drugs, the approach has been to fight drug abuse and addiction by clamping down on offenders. The thinking was that a get-tough approach would deter would-be drug abusers from using, and in the process, this would help prevent addiction. Whether this strategy was ever effective is a matter of opinion, but it has become especially controversial in recent years. America's prisons are overcrowded, too many nonviolent drug offenders are behind bars, and the heroin problem continues to grow worse. Thus, more and more people are suggesting that a different strategy might be needed. Lauren-Brooke Eisen, who is counsel in the Justice Program at New York University School of Law's Brennan Center for Justice, shares her thoughts in a February 2014 article titled "How to Fight the Heroin Epidemic":

> **America's prisons are overcrowded, too many nonviolent drug offenders are behind bars, and the heroin problem continues to grow worse.**

The reactionary "tough on crime" rhetoric led us astray. It resulted in policymakers enacting ineffective and overly punitive drug policies. . . . Today, almost half of all federal inmates are in prison for drug crimes and 1 in 5 state prisoners are serving sentences for drug crimes. They are part of the world's largest and most expensive prison population, which since 1980 has increased by more than 800%. In the last 40 years, federal and state governments have spent more than $1 trillion on the "war on drugs." What we now know is that drug use should be treated as a public health issue, rather than just a criminal justice issue.[63]

A Shift in Focus

Eisen goes on to cite some statistics related to the focus on punishing drug addicts rather than helping them recover and stay clean. "Each prisoner costs taxpayers an average of $30,000 a year," she says, "money that could be better spent on drug treatment programs with a stronger record of success." Eisen goes on to say that treatment has been shown to not only save taxpayer dollars but also to reduce crime and reduce recidivism (relapse into drug-related crime after being punished) fifteen times more effectively than law enforcement alone. "As illegal drug use again becomes a focus of public policy," she says, "it is vital that we don't make the same mistakes that created mass incarceration in America. Decades of experience have given us the tools to do better. It is now incumbent on policymakers, from the White House to state legislatures, to apply those lessons."[64]

Eric Holder shares the perspective that America's heroin problem cannot be solved by law enforcement alone. In a March 2014 statement before the US Sentencing Commission, Holder vowed that the US Department of Justice was committed to combating the heroin epidemic through a combination of law enforcement and treatment. In a move that refuted the decades-long practice of mandatory minimum sentences for drug offenses, Holder called for reduced sentences for defendants in most drug cases. One benefit of this strategy would be reducing the burgeoning prison population in the United States. "Certain types of cases result in too many Americans going to prison for far too long," says Holder, "and at times for no truly good public safety reason. Although the United States comprises just five percent of the world's population, we incarcerate almost a quarter of the world's prisoners."[65]

Holder adds that the stiffest drug-related punishments would be reserved for those who commit the worst drug trafficking offenses, and the benefits of doing so would be immense. "By reserving the most severe penalties for dangerous and violent drug traffickers," he says, "we can better protect public safety, deterrence and rehabilitation while saving billions of dollars and strengthening communities."[66] Justice Department officials estimate that Holder's policy changes are expected to reduce America's prison population by 6,550 people within five years and result in a 17 percent decrease in the average length of time incarcerated drug offenders serve.

> " Eric Holder shares the perspective that America's heroin problem cannot be solved by law enforcement alone. "

Ready for a Change

According to a 2014 national survey by the Pew Research Center, the majority of Americans agree with shifting away from punishing heroin addicts in favor of a treatment-based approach. When asked what the government should focus on in terms of its drug policies, 67 percent of the 1,821 survey participants said the focus should be on providing treatment for Americans who use illicit drugs such as heroin and cocaine. Only 26 percent said they wanted the government to focus on prosecuting illicit drug users. The report states: "The public appears ready for a truce in the long-running war on drugs."[67]

A major shift in perspective was evident in the survey when participants were asked for their opinions on mandatory minimum sentences. Specifically, they were asked whether it was a good or bad thing that some states were beginning to move away from mandatory sentencing for nonviolent drug offenders. During a 2001 Pew Research survey 47 percent of respondents had said it was good that some states had moved away from mandatory minimum sentences; by 2014 that number had risen to 63 percent. "As a growing number of states ease penalties for drug possession," the report authors write, "the public expresses increasingly positive views of the move away from mandatory sentences for non-violent drug crimes."[68]

Heroin Abuse Prevention

As top law enforcement officials wrestle with how to stop heroin abuse in the United States, communities across the country are working at the local level to develop heroin prevention programs. Surveys have shown that the general public is largely unaware of how widespread the country's heroin problem is or how much addictions have spiked in recent years. Nor do many people know about the connection between abuse of prescription pain drugs and heroin use and addiction. Public education campaigns, much like those designed to reduce smoking or prevent drunk driving, could help people better understand heroin addiction, how much the problem has grown, and the warning signs to watch for in order to prevent it from happening to them or a loved one.

Students in Naperville, Illinois, have developed a prevention program for other students. Like many other suburban communities, Naperville has developed a serious heroin problem in recent years. A major reason is the city's proximity to Chicago, which has one of the worst heroin problems in the United States. A route known as the "Heroin Highway" connects people from Naperville directly to the drug suppliers on Chicago's west side. "Every suburban community along [that route] is at risk and has their own issues because of that," says Kathleen M. Burke, CEO of the Robert Crown Center for Health Education. "I believe police are finding that it used to be you go to the West Side of Chicago. Now there are stops in between that have developed for distribution."[69]

In 2011 six teens and young adults from Naperville died from heroin-related causes, including three students who attended Neuqua Valley High School. At about that same time, school social worker Pam Witt had a disturbing conversation with a couple of high school juniors. They were nonchalantly telling her about how they had driven to Chicago to buy heroin, as she explains: "These little girls who look like cheerleaders, they'd tell me how they'd get into a car, drive down I-290, exit at the K streets and pull into an alley. They'd park, and sooner or later, somebody would knock on their car window. They'd hand over $100 bucks and they'd get 12 bags of heroin. It was crazy. It was scary. It was so, so scary." Between what she had heard from the girls and the tragic overdose deaths, Witt knew action was needed. "We knew we needed to do something," she says, "and we knew we needed to do it right."[70]

> **Public education campaigns, much like those designed to reduce smoking or prevent drunk driving, could help people better understand heroin addiction.**

Witt and the high school's other three social workers came up with a strategy: Rather than creating a program and then presenting it to students, they went to the students first to gather their input. The social workers asked questions about what the teens would actually listen to and "What won't you roll your eyes at?"[71] The end result of these and other conversations was a student-led heroin prevention program called Confront the Elephant. The name comes from the metaphorical expression, "elephant in the room," which refers to an obvious truth that is either being ignored or going unaddressed. In this case, heroin is the "elephant."

At Neuqua Valley High School, seniors develop and lead their own Confront the Elephant programs. "There are no teachers or administrators on stage. And there's no eye-rolling in the teenage audience, either,"

> **Heroin addiction in the United States has proved to be a formidable problem—one that no one believes will be easy to solve.**

writes Mary Ellen Flannery in a March 2014 *NEA Today* article. "Former heroin users, sometimes Neuqua Valley students, as well as the mother and sister of one of those 2011 heroin victims, speak in small groups to their freshman peers." Confront the Elephant also includes a blue-ribbon health program for sophomores, which involves several weeks of drug prevention lessons and activities and periodic training and information sessions for parents of high school students. The program, according to students, social workers, and administrators, has been a rousing success. "Today, three years after she and her colleagues confronted the elephant," says Flannery, "Witt doesn't hear so many of those stories"[72] about students driving to Chicago to buy heroin.

The Fly Effect

In September 2013, as Wisconsin's heroin addiction rates and incidents of overdose were growing to alarming levels, the state's Department of Justice launched a full-scale public awareness campaign. It was dubbed The Fly Effect, a name that was inspired by the children's nursery rhyme whose lyrics start with, "There was an old lady who swallowed a fly." Advertising executive DeAnna DeCaluwe explains how the nursery rhyme concept parallels the awareness message: "In the rhyme, after the woman swallows the fly, she swallows a spider to catch the fly, and a host of other animals, each to catch the last, until she swallows a horse (and dies, of course). The Fly Effect campaign, which was inspired by the nursery rhyme, brings to life the downward spiral and destructive power of heroin. The premise of The Fly Effect is that 'sometimes the biggest spirals have the smallest start.' Research has shown that 75% of those who try [heroin] actually re-use the drug."[73]

One young woman who is featured in The Fly Effect campaign is Julie, who is serving time in prison for drug-related first-degree reckless homicide. Because of her own experience, and also having watched friends overdose on heroin, she says that public awareness of the problem is critical. In a video that features her, Julie makes it clear that heroin robs addicts of everything that is important to them: "It changes you into a monster that you don't even know. You look in the mirror, and you don't even know who you are, and that's [the] reality with drugs. It's not fun, and it's not a party. It's not, 'Oh, we're just going to try this once, and that's it.' Don't even go there. Don't even tempt fate."[74]

A Future of Uncertainty

Heroin addiction in the United States has proved to be a formidable problem—one that no one believes will be easy to solve. It has become clear to many in law enforcement, including those holding the country's top positions, that the get-tough approach to fighting drug abuse is not enough to fight addiction. "While smart law enforcement will always play a critical role in protecting communities from drug crime," says Holder, "we will never be able to arrest or incarcerate our way to becoming a safer nation."[75] The proper strategy, according to Holder and innumerable others who share his views, is to create and enact education and awareness programs that help prevent heroin abuse, as well as to focus on treating heroin addicts rather than punishing them.

What Can Be Done About Heroin Addiction?

"We can only hope that the sympathy shown to white, often affluent, young heroin users will add momentum to the calls to roll back the wasteful incarceration policies that hurt the country as a whole and have disproportionately impacted communities of color."

—Stephen Lerner and Nelini Stamp, "When Heroin Use Hit the Suburbs, Everything Changed," Opinions, *Washington Post*, May 16, 2014. www.washingtonpost.com.

Lerner is a fellow at Georgetown University's Kalmanovitz Initiative and the architect of the Justice for Janitors campaign, and Stamp is the youth engagement director for Working Families.

"The administration must make a stronger effort to prioritize treatment programs as a solution to drug crises, including the current heroin epidemic."

—Lauren-Brooke Eisen, "How to Fight the Heroin Epidemic," MSNBC, February 23, 2014. www.msnbc.com.

Eisen is counsel in the Justice Program at the New York University School of Law.

Bracketed quotes indicate conflicting positions.

* Editor's Note: While the definition of a primary source can be narrowly or broadly defined, for the purposes of Compact Research, a primary source consists of: 1) results of original research presented by an organization or researcher; 2) eyewitness accounts of events, personal experience, or work experience; 3) first-person editorials offering pundits' opinions; 4) government officials presenting political plans and/or policies; 5) representatives of organizations presenting testimony or policy.

66 **Ninety percent of people who need help never receive it. Indeed, people with addiction are more likely to wind up in prison than in rehab.** 99

—David Sheff, *Clean: Overcoming Addiction and Ending America's Greatest Tragedy*. New York: Houghton Mifflin Harcourt, 2013, p. 15.

Sheff is a journalist and author whose son, Nic, has battled addiction to numerous drugs, including heroin and crystal meth.

66 **There should be just as many public service announcements about addiction as there are Viagra and Cialis commercials.** 99

—Steven Kassels, "The Scourge of Heroin Addiction," Opinion, *Boston Globe*, April 1, 2014. www.bostonglobe.com.

Kassels is an addiction specialist who serves as medical director of Community Substance Abuse Centers in Westfield, Massachusetts.

66 **Addiction is a medical condition, yet there is little sympathy because society views it to be self-inflicted.** 99

—Tracey Helton Mitchell, "I Went from Heroin Addict to PTA Mom," CNN, February 4, 2014. www.cnn.com.

Mitchell is a woman from San Francisco who overcame an eight-year addiction to heroin.

66 **We need to start another war on drugs. This is a war that needs to be fought with resources and commitment from our leaders, because if we lose this war, we might permanently change the face of our society.** 99

—Manny Alvarez, "Dr. Manny: Heroin on the Rise: Cheap, Available, and Out of Control," Fox News, August 1, 2013. www.foxnews.com.

Alvarez is a physician who serves as Fox News's senior managing editor for health news.

❝The translation of scientific findings in drug abuse into prevention and treatment initiatives clearly requires partnership with federal agencies.❞

—Nora D. Volkow, "Harnessing the Power of Science to Inform Substance Abuse and Addiction Policy and Practice," testimony to Congress, April 2, 2014. www.drugabuse.gov.

Volkow is director of the National Institute on Drug Abuse.

....

❝Americans will always use heroin. In order to keep them safe, providing the best available public health information seems the responsible and ethical thing to do.❞

—Carl L. Hart, "Heroin (Alone) Is Not the Problem," *Huffington Post*, July 19, 2013. www.huffingtonpost.com.

Hart is a neuroscientist at Columbia University in New York City.

....

❝Drug addiction is a preventable disease. Results from NIDA-funded research have shown that prevention programs involving families, schools, communities, and the media are effective in reducing drug abuse.❞

—National Institute on Drug Abuse (NIDA), "Understanding Drug Abuse and Addiction," *Drug Facts*, November 2012. www.drugabuse.gov.

An agency of the National Institutes of Health, the NIDA seeks to end drug abuse and addiction in the United States.

....

Facts and Illustrations

What Can Be Done About Heroin Addiction?

- According to Westfield, Massachusetts, substance abuse specialist Steven Kassels, it costs at least **$50,000 per year** to incarcerate a drug addict compared with approximately **$5,000 per year** for outpatient drug treatment.

- A September 2013 SAMHSA report shows that in 2012 **75.9 percent** of teens reported having seen or heard drug or alcohol prevention messages from sources outside of school.

- According to US attorney general Eric Holder, due to increased DEA investigations the amount of heroin seized along America's southwest border has increased by more than **320 percent** since 2008.

- The Drug Policy Alliance says that more than **1.5 million** people in the United States were arrested in 2012 for nonviolent drug offenses.

- According to assistant secretary of state William Brownfield, US law enforcement has gotten better at interrupting the flow of methamphetamine and cocaine from Latin America, but the amount of pure heroin entering the country has doubled over the past four years.

- Between 2009 and 2011, while the Project Lazarus prevention program was in place in Wilkes County, North Carolina, there was a **69 percent** decline in opioid overdose rates.

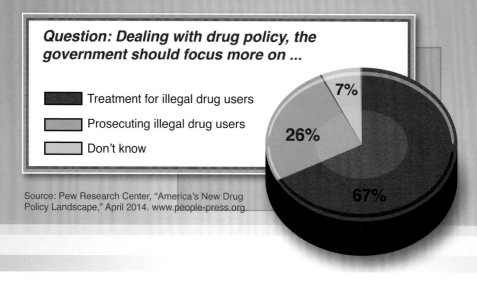

Americans Want Addicts Treated, Not Punished

In April 2014 the Pew Research Center released a national survey that was designed to evaluate Americans' opinions about the government's drug policies. As the chart shows, when asked whether the focus should be on prosecution or treatment of illegal drug users, 67 percent chose the latter.

Question: Dealing with drug policy, the government should focus more on ...

- Treatment for illegal drug users
- Prosecuting illegal drug users
- Don't know

7%

26%

67%

Source: Pew Research Center, "America's New Drug Policy Landscape," April 2014. www.people-press.org.

- Gil Kerlikowske, director of the White House Office of National Drug Control Policy, reports that his agency at one time had **$190 million** for drug prevention programs, but the allocation was eliminated by Congress.

- According to the Drug Policy Alliance, there are more than **115,000** methadone maintenance patients in the United States, including **40,000** in New York State and **20,000** in California.

- In a November 2013 survey by YouGov and Huffington Post, **86 percent** of Americans said they did not want heroin to be legalized.

Legalization Not the Answer

Addiction experts, health officials, and law enforcement professionals agree that something must be done to address the heroin problem in the United States—but how it should be solved is an issue of debate. One possible solution is legalization: advocates say legalization of heroin would put the emphasis on addiction treatment rather than criminalization. According to a November 25, 2013 YouGov/*Huffington Post* poll, however, a large number of Americans do not agree with that approach.

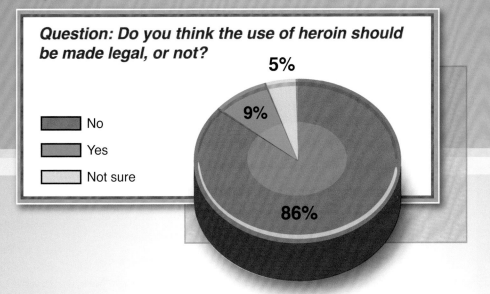

Question: Do you think the use of heroin should be made legal, or not?

- No
- Yes
- Not sure

5%

9%

86%

Source: Peter Moore, "Poll Results: Drug Penalties," YouGov, November 25, 2013. http://today.yougov.com.

- According to Harm Reduction Coalition executive director Allan Clear, if the United States adopted an addiction maintenance program, with heroin administered in a controlled clinical setting for treatment-resistant addicts, many people's lives could be saved.

- In a November 2013 survey by YouGov and Huffington Post, **more than half** of respondents said that someone who is caught with a small amount of heroin, and has no prior convictions, should not be sentenced to prison.

Key People and Advocacy Groups

Friedrich Bayer: A German dye salesman who, along with Johann Friedrich Weskott, founded Friedr. Bayer et comp, a partnership that eventually became Bayer & Company, one of the world's leading pharmaceutical organizations. In 1898 Bayer began marketing and selling heroin for medicinal use.

Max Bockmühl and Gustav Ehrhart: German chemists who synthesized methadone in 1937 while searching for a pain-killing drug that was less addictive than morphine.

Drug Enforcement Administration (DEA): The United States' leading law enforcement agency for combating the sale and distribution of narcotics and other illegal drugs.

Foundation for a Drug-Free World: An organization that seeks to empower youth and adults with factual information about drugs so they can make informed decisions and live drug free.

Francis Burton Harrison: A US congressman from New York who strongly favored the prohibition of heroin and other addictive drugs; he authored the Harrison Narcotics Tax Act, which became law in December 1914.

Narconon International: An organization that helps people who are addicted to drugs by providing educational information and rehabilitation programs.

Narcotics Anonymous: A fellowship of recovering drug addicts that seeks to help people for whom drugs have become a major problem.

National Institute on Drug Abuse (NIDA): An agency of the National Institutes of Health that seeks to end drug abuse and addiction in the United States.

Richard M. Nixon: The thirty-seventh president of the United States and chief creator of the "war on drugs," which began in 1971.

Friedrich Wilhelm Sertürner: A German apprentice pharmacist who, in 1805, became the first to create morphine by combining opium with chemicals; decades passed before scientists learned that morphine can be used to make heroin.

Substance Abuse and Mental Health Services Administration (SAMHSA): An agency of the US government that works to improve the quality and availability of substance abuse prevention, alcohol and drug addiction treatment, and mental health services.

Arnold S. Trebach and Kevin Zeese: In 1987 Trebach, a professor at American University, and Zeese, an attorney, founded the Drug Policy Foundation, which they described as the "loyal opposition to the war on drugs."

Charles Romley Alder Wright: An English researcher who in 1874 combined morphine with acetic anhydride to create diacetylmorphine, which later became known as heroin.

Chronology

1805
German apprentice pharmacist Friedrich Wilhelm Sertürner dissolves opium in acid and adds ammonia to the mixture, creating a crystalline substance that later becomes known as morphine.

1897
Scientists at the German pharmaceutical company Bayer test diacetylmorphine on animals and on Bayer employees, who report that it makes them feel strong, even heroic; hence, the drug is renamed heroin and Bayer starts manufacturing it.

1914
US president Woodrow Wilson signs the Harrison Narcotics Tax Act into law, which specifies that only physicians and pharmacists may buy, sell, and dispense heroin and other opiates.

1924
With passage of the Heroin Act, the US government bans the importation, distribution, and all use of heroin in the United States, including for medicinal purposes; addicts begin buying heroin from illegal street dealers.

1800 1875 1900 1925 1950

1874
English researcher Charles Romley Alder Wright combines morphine with acetic anhydride and cooks the mixture on a stove. His creation is diacetylmorphine (later called heroin).

1898
The Bayer Company begins distribution of heroin and launches an aggressive advertising campaign, marketing it as a cough, chest, and lung medicine.

1937
While searching for a painkilling drug that is less addictive than morphine, German chemists Max Bockmühl and Gustav Ehrhart create a synthetic substance later known as methadone.

1913
After receiving hundreds of reports of overdoses due to nonmedical use, the Bayer Company ends its production of heroin; users turn to illegal channels for obtaining the drug.

1903
Physician George E. Pettey publishes an article in the *Alabama Medical Journal* titled "The Heroin Habit: Another Curse," in which he describes heroin as an addictive drug.

1964

Research by physician Vincent P. Dole shows that methadone is effective in treating people who suffer from heroin addiction by reducing withdrawal symptoms.

1971

President Richard M. Nixon declares a "war on drugs" by dramatically increasing the size and presence of federal drug control agencies and toughening penalties for drug-related offenses.

2002

The US Food and Drug Administration approves the use of an opioid called buprenorphine for prescription by physicians to treat patients with heroin addiction.

2014

The US Food and Drug Administration approves a handheld injection tool that can deliver a lifesaving antidote drug known as naloxone to people who have overdosed on heroin.

1960   1980   2000

1970

The Comprehensive Drug Abuse Prevention and Control Act (Controlled Substances Act) divides drugs into five categories known as schedules, sets regulations, and lists penalties for distribution or possession of narcotics and other "dangerous drugs."

1973

President Richard M. Nixon issues an executive order that establishes the Drug Enforcement Administration (DEA).

1972

Researchers from Johns Hopkins University discover that neurons in the human brain have specific receptor sites for the opioid drugs: opium, heroin, morphine, and codeine; this enhances scientific understanding of how drug addiction works.

1997

Federal data show that more than 400,000 people are behind bars for nonviolent drug offenses, a substantial increase from 50,000 in 1980.

2012

The number of Americans meeting the criteria for heroin dependence or abuse reaches 467,000, a figure that has more than doubled since 2002.

2010

A report by the United Nations Office on Drugs and Crime shows that more than 15 million people worldwide consume illicit opiates, with the majority using heroin.

Related Organizations

Common Sense for Drug Policy

1377-C Spencer Ave.
Lancaster, PA 17603
phone: (717) 299-0600
e-mail: info@csdp.org • website: www.csdp.org

In an effort to reform drug policy in the United States, Common Sense for Drug Policy disseminates information and comments on existing laws, policies, and practices. Its website offers a wide variety of information related to addiction and drugs.

Drug Enforcement Administration (DEA)

800 K St., NW, Suite 500,
Washington, DC 20001
phone: (202) 305-8500
website: www.justice.gov

The DEA is the United States' top federal drug law enforcement agency. Its website links to a separate site called "Just Think Twice" that is designed for teenagers and features fact sheets, personal experiences, and numerous publications specifically about heroin addiction.

Drug Free America Foundation

5999 Central Ave., Suite 301
Saint Petersburg, FL 33710
phone: (727) 828-0211 • fax: (727) 828-0212
e-mail: webmaster@dfaf.org • website: www.dfaf.org

The Drug Free America Foundation is a drug prevention and policy organization. Its website has a search engine that produces numerous articles about heroin, and it also has links to a site created for young people titled Students Taking Action Not Drugs (STAND).

Drug Policy Alliance

131 W. Thirty-Third St., 15th Floor
New York, NY 10001
phone: (212) 613-8020 • fax: (212) 613-8021
e-mail: nyc@drugpolicy.org • website: www.drugpolicy.org

The Drug Policy Alliance promotes alternatives to current drug policy that are grounded in science, compassion, health, and human rights. Its website features drug facts, statistics, information about drug laws and individual rights, and a search engine that produces numerous articles about heroin abuse and addiction.

Foundation for a Drug-Free World

1626 N. Wilcox Ave., Suite 1297
Los Angeles, CA 90028
phone: (818) 952-5260; toll-free: (888) 668-6378
e-mail: info@drugfreeworld.org • website: www.drugfreeworld.org

The Foundation for a Drug-Free World exists to empower youth and adults with factual information about drugs so they can make informed decisions and live drug free. A wealth of information about heroin is available on its interactive website, including videos, fact sheets, educational booklets, and personal stories of young people who have fought heroin addiction.

Narconon International

4652 Hollywood Blvd.
Los Angeles, CA 90027
phone: (323) 962-2404 • fax: (323) 962-6872
e-mail: info@narconon.org • website: www.narconon.org

Founded in 1965 by a man who was incarcerated at Arizona State Prison, Narconon International helps people who are addicted to drugs by providing educational information and rehabilitation programs. Many good articles about heroin and addiction can be found on its website.

National Institute on Drug Abuse (NIDA)

National Institutes of Health
6001 Executive Blvd., Room 5213
Bethesda, MD 20892-9561
phone: (301) 443-1124
e-mail: information@nida.nih.gov • website: www.drugabuse.gov

The NIDA supports research efforts and ensures the rapid dissemination of research to improve drug abuse prevention, treatment, and policy. The website links to a separate "NIDA for Teens" site, which is designed especially for teenagers and provides a wealth of information about illicit drugs (including heroin) and addiction.

Office of National Drug Control Policy

750 Seventeenth St. NW
Washington, DC 20503
phone: (800) 666-3332 • fax: (202) 395–6708
e-mail: ondcp@ncjrs.org • website: www.whitehouse.gov/ondcp

A component of the Executive Office of the President, the Office of National Drug Control Policy is responsible for directing the federal government's antidrug programs. A wealth of information about heroin can be produced through the website's search engine.

Partnership at Drugfree.org (formerly Partnership for a Drug-Free America)

352 Park Ave. South, 9th Floor
New York, NY 10010
phone: (212) 922-1560 • fax: (212) 922-1570
website: www.drugfree.org

The Partnership at Drugfree.org is dedicated to helping parents and families solve the problem of teenage substance abuse. Its website offers a large number of informative publications that can be accessed through the search engine.

Substance Abuse and Mental Health Services Administration (SAMHSA)

1 Choke Cherry Rd.
Rockville, MD 20857
phone: (877) 726-4727
e-mail: SAMHSAInfo@samhsa.hhs.gov • website: www.samhsa.gov

The SAMHSA's mission is to reduce the impact of substance abuse and mental illness on America's communities. The site offers a wealth of information about substance abuse and numerous publications related to heroin are available through its search engine.

For Further Research

Books

Taite Adams, *Opiate Addiction: The Painkiller Addiction Epidemic, Heroin Addiction and the Way Out*. St. Petersburg, FL: Rapid Response, 2013.

Michael W. Clune, *White Out: The Secret Life of Heroin*. Center City, MN: Hazelden, 2013.

Joani Gammill, *Painkillers, Heroin, and the Road to Sanity*. Center City, MN: Hazelden, 2014.

Joe Putignano, *Acrobaddict*. Las Vegas, NV: Central Recovery, 2013.

David Sheff, *Clean: Overcoming Addiction and Ending America's Greatest Tragedy*. New York: Houghton Mifflin Harcourt, 2013.

Barry Spunt, *Heroin and Music in New York City*. New York: Palgrave Macmillan, 2014.

Jerry Stahl, *The Heroin Chronicles*. New York: Akashic, 2013.

Periodicals

George Chuvalo, "Lost Boys," *Toronto Life*, November 2013.

Jeff Deeney, "Hoffman and the Terrible Heroin Deaths in the Shadows," *Atlantic*, January/February 2014.

David DiSalvo, "Why Is Heroin Abuse Rising While Other Drug Abuse Is Falling?," *Forbes*, January 14, 2014.

J. David Goodman and Michael Wilson, "Heroin's New Home Town," *New York Times*, May 4, 2014.

Eliza Gray, "Heroin Gains Popularity as Cheap Doses Flood the U.S.," *Time*, February 4, 2014.

Christy Gutowski, Gregory Pratt, and Matthew Walberg, "Heroin: The Human Toll," *Chicago Tribune*, September 21, 2013.

Kristina Lindborg, "Why Heroin Is Spreading in America's Suburbs," *Christian Science Monitor*, March 23, 2014.

Christa Parravani, interview by Angela Ledgerwood, "I Lost My Identical Twin," *Cosmopolitan*, March 2013.

Matt Pearce and Tina Susman, "Philip Seymour Hoffman's Death Calls Attention to Rise in Heroin Use," *Los Angeles Times*, February 3, 2014.

Julia Rubin, "How Heroin Is Invading America's Schools," *Teen Vogue*, January 2, 2014.

Julia Savacool, "Ivy League Overdose," *Cosmopolitan*, November 2013.

Deborah Sontag, "Portrait of a Heroin Victim," *New York Times Upfront*, April 21, 2014.

Jacob Sullum, "Does Calling Heroin Addiction a Brain Disease Help Avoid Tragedies Like Philip Seymour Hoffman's Death?," *Forbes*, February 2014.

Susan Svriuga, "Fairfax Mother of Young Heroin Addict: 'There Were Clues. But We Had No Clue,'" *Washington Post*, April 22, 2014.

Michelle Tauber, "A Life Cut Short: Cory Monteith: 1982–2013," *People*, July 29, 2013.

Internet Sources

Ronni Berke and Poppy Harlow, "One Snapshot in a Tragic National Picture: Long Island Sees Exploding Heroin Use," CNN, February 9, 2014. www.cnn.com/2014/02/07/us/long-island-heroin-youths.

Linda Carroll, "Hooked: A Teacher's Addiction and the New Face of Heroin," Today Health, April 8, 2014. www.today.com/health/hooked-teachers-addiction-new-face-heroin-2D79496263.

A. Thomas McLellan, "Dying of a Heroin Overdose Does Not Make You a Scumbag," blog, *Huffington Post*, April 27, 2014. www.huffingtonpost.com/a-thomas-mclellan-phd/philip-seymour-hoffman_b_4789867.html.

Seth Mnookin, "Why Philip Seymour Hoffman's Death Is So Scary," *Slate*, February 4, 2014. www.slate.com/articles/health_and_science/medical_examiner/2014/02/philip_seymour_hoffman_s_drug_death_the_science_of_addiction_recovery_and.html.

National Institute on Drug Abuse (NIDA), *Heroin*, Research Report Series, 2014. www.drugabuse.gov/sites/default/files/rrheroin_4_14 .pdf.

New York Times, "Lowering the Deadly Cost of Drug Abuse," Room for Debate, March 17, 2014. www.nytimes.com/room fordebate/2014/03/17/lowering-the-deadly-cost-of-drug-abuse.

Matt Taylor, "Heroin Threatens Vermont's Rural Paradise," *Newsweek* Daily Beast, February 19, 2014. www.thedailybeast.com/articles/2014 /02/19/heroin-threatens-vermont-s-rural-paradise.html.

Source Notes

Overview

1. Ben Cimons, "A Suburban Heroin Addict Describes His Brush with Death and His Hopes for a Better Life," *Washington Post*, February 7, 2014. www.washingtonpost.com.
2. Cimons, "A Suburban Heroin Addict Describes His Brush with Death and His Hopes for a Better Life."
3. Cimons, "A Suburban Heroin Addict Describes His Brush with Death and His Hopes for a Better Life."
4. National Institute on Drug Abuse, "Heroin," *Drug Facts*, April 2013. www.drugabuse.gov.
5. National Institute on Drug Abuse, *Heroin*, Research Report Series, April 2014. www.drugabuse.gov.
6. Quoted in Ronni Berke and Poppy Harlow, "One Snapshot in a Tragic National Picture: Long Island Sees Exploding Heroin Use," CNN, February 9, 2014. www.cnn.com.
7. James B. Comey, "Many FBI Field Offices Are Seeing Heroin Problems," in *Subject to Debate*, March/April 2014. www.policeforum.org.
8. US Drug Enforcement Administration, "National Drug Threat Assessment Summary," November 2013. www.justice.gov.
9. Quoted in Susan Svrluga, "Fairfax Mother of Young Heroin Addict: 'There Were Clues. But We Had No Clue,'" *Washington Post*, April 22, 2014. www.washingtonpost.com.
10. National Institute on Drug Abuse, *Heroin*, Research Report Series.
11. Quoted in Susan Brink, "How Heroin Kills: What Might Have Happened to Philip Seymour Hoffman," *National Geographic*, February 4, 2014. http://news.nationalgeographic.com.
12. Narconon International, "10 Signs and Symptoms of Heroin Abuse," *Narconon—Drug Addiction and Recovery Blog*. www.narconon.org.
13. Narconon International, "10 Signs of Hidden Heroin Addiction," November 12, 2013. www.narconon.org.
14. Foundation for a Drug-Free World, "The Truth About Heroin." www.drugfreeworld.org.
15. Narconon International, "Heroin's Damage to Lungs and Heart." www.narconon.org.
16. Narconon International, "Heroin's Damage to Lungs and Heart."
17. Carl L. Hart, "Heroin (Alone) Is Not the Problem," *Huffington Post*, July 19, 2013. www.huffingtonpost.com.
18. Quoted in Brianna Gurciullo, "Law Student Died from Lethal Mix of Heroin, Adderall," *GW Hatchet*, March 7, 2013. www.gwhatchet.com.
19. Quoted in Chris Curtis, "What Happens When Heroin Hijacks the Brain?," *Recorder* (Greenfield, MA), May 4, 2014. www.recorder.com.
20. Nora D. Volkow, "Harnessing the Power of Science to Inform Substance Abuse and Addiction Policy and Practice," testimony to Congress, April 2, 2014. www.drugabuse.gov.
21. Volkow, "Harnessing the Power of Science to Inform Substance Abuse and Addiction Policy and Practice."

How Serious a Problem Is Heroin Addiction?

22. Comey, "Many FBI Field Offices Are Seeing Heroin Problems."

23. Eric Holder, "Attorney General Eric Holder Delivers Remarks at the 2014 Police Executive Research Forum," US Department of Justice, April 16, 2014. www.justice.gov.

24. Michele Leonhart, "Young People Think Drug Abuse Is Not Harmful," in *Subject to Debate*, March/April 2014. www.policeforum.org.

25. Theodore J. Cicero, Matthew S. Ellis, Hilary L. Surratt, and Steven P. Kurtz, "The Changing Face of Heroin Use in the United States: A Retrospective Analysis of the Past 50 Years," *JAMA Psychiatry*, May 2014. http://archpsyc.jamanetwork.com.

26. Cicero, Ellis, Surratt, and Kurtz, "The Changing Face of Heroin Use in the United States."

27. Quoted in Alice G. Walton, "On Heroin: More Users White and Suburban than Ever Before," *Forbes*, May 28, 2014. www.forbes.com.

28. Andrew Welsh-Huggins, "A Look at Heroin Use, Deaths, in Some US States," *Big Story*, AP, April 5, 2014. http://bigstory.ap.org.

29. Scott Thomson, "Most Fatal ODs in Camden Are from Out of Town," in *Subject to Debate*, March/April 2014. www.policeforum.org.

30. Quoted in Amy Forliti, Dan Sewell, and Nigel Duara, "'We're All Paying': Heroin Spreads Misery in US," *Big Story*, AP, April 5, 2014. http://bigstory.ap.org.

31. Quoted in Forliti, Sewell, and Duara, "'We're All Paying.'"

32. Quoted in Katharine Q. Seelye, "Heroin Scourge Overtakes a 'Quaint' Vermont Town," *New York Times*, March 5, 2014. www.nytimes.com.

33. Peter Shumlin, "Gov. Shumlin's 2014 State of the State Address," January 8, 2014. http://governor.vermont.gov.

34. Gina Tron, "How Did Idyllic Vermont Become America's Heroin Capital?," *Politico Magazine*, February 7, 2014. www.politico.com.

35. Tron, "How Did Idyllic Vermont Become America's Heroin Capital?"

36. Quoted in Kevin Johnson, "Heroin a Growing Threat Across USA, Police Say," *USA Today*, April 17, 2014. www.usatoday.com.

What Are the Health Risks of Heroin Addiction?

37. Brian Rinker, "Viral VICE Article on Tenderloin Drug Use Elicits Criticism," *My Heroin Years* (blog), March 9, 2013. www.brianrinkerreporting.com.

38. Brian Rinker, "Past Heroin Addict Tells Abscess Horror Stories," *Golden Gate Xpress* (San Francisco), May 18, 2013. www.goldengatexpress.org.

39. Rinker, "Past Heroin Addict Tells Abscess Horror Stories."

40. Rinker, "Past Heroin Addict Tells Abscess Horror Stories."

41. National Institute on Drug Abuse, *Heroin*, Research Report Series.

42. National Institute on Drug Abuse, *Heroin*, Research Report Series.

43. US Department of Health and Human Services, "Hepatitis C Virus Infection in Young Persons Who Inject Drugs," May 29, 2013. http://aids.gov.

44. Centers for Disease Control and Prevention, "Hepatitis C Virus Infection Among Adolescents and Young Adults—Massachusetts, 2002–2009," *Morbidity and Mortality Weekly Report*, May 6, 2011. www.cdc.gov.

45. National Institute on Drug Abuse, "Heroin," *Drug Facts*.

46. Quoted in Society for Neuroscience, "Brains of Heroin Users Change with Years of Addiction," November 10, 2013. www.sfn.org.

47. March of Dimes, "Heroin and Pregnancy," November 2013. www.marchofdimes.com.

48. University of Rochester Medical Center, "Neonatal Abstinence Syndrome," 2014. www.urmc.rochester.edu.

49. Quoted in Jen Christensen, "How Heroin Kills You," CNN, February 4, 2014. www.cnn.com.
50. Brian Rinker, "New Laws Affect the Consequences of Calling in an Overdose," *My Heroin Years* (blog), March 25, 2013. www.brianrinkerreporting.com/2013/03/25/706.
51. Rinker, "New Laws Affect the Consequences of Calling in an Overdose."

Can People Overcome Heroin Addiction?

52. Quoted in Liz Neporent, "Why Philip Seymour Hoffman's 23 Years of Sobriety Didn't Mean He Kicked the Habit," ABC News, February 4, 2014. http://abcnews.go.com.
53. Quoted in Neporent, "Why Philip Seymour Hoffman's 23 Years of Sobriety Didn't Mean He Kicked the Habit."
54. Philip Seymour Hoffman, interview by Steve Kroft, *60 Minutes*, CBS News, June 14, 2006. www.cbsnews.com.
55. National Institute on Drug Abuse, "DrugFacts: Treatment Approaches for Drug Addiction," September 2009. www.drugabuse.gov.
56. National Institute on Drug Abuse, "DrugFacts: Treatment Approaches for Drug Addiction," September 2009.
57. Quoted in Berke and Harlow, "One Snapshot in a Tragic National Picture."
58. Quoted in Berke and Harlow, "One Snapshot in a Tragic National Picture."
59. Quoted in Tracey Samuelson, "Heroin, Opiate Addicts Find It Tough to Get Treatment," Marketplace, May 27, 2014. www.marketplace.org.
60. Quoted in Forliti, Sewell, and Duara, "'We're All Paying.'"
61. Quoted in Forliti, Sewell, and Duara, "'We're All Paying.'"
62. Quoted in Forliti, Sewell, and Duara, "'We're All Paying.'"

What Can Be Done About Heroin Addiction?

63. Lauren-Brooke Eisen, "How to Fight the Heroin Epidemic," MSNBC, February 23, 2014. www.msnbc.com.
64. Eisen, "How to Fight the Heroin Epidemic."
65. Quoted in Sari Horwitz, "Holder Calls for Reduced Sentences for Low-Level Drug Offenders," *Washington Post*, March 13, 2014. www.washingtonpost.com.
66. Quoted in Horwitz, "Holder Calls for Reduced Sentences for Low-Level Drug Offenders."
67. Pew Research Center, "America's New Drug Policy Landscape," April 2, 2014. www.people-press.org.
68. Pew Research Center, "America's New Drug Policy Landscape."
69. Quoted in Melissa Jenco, "Naperville Parents Who Lost Daughter to Heroin Try to Educate Other Kids, Parents," *Chicago Tribune*, March 12, 2012. http://articles.chicagotribune.com.
70. Quoted in Mary Ellen Flannery, "School Prevention Programs Try to Rein in Heroin, Pill Epidemic," *NEA Today*, March 21, 2014. www.neatoday.org.
71. Quoted in Flannery, "School Prevention Programs Try to Rein in Heroin, Pill Epidemic."
72. Flannery, "School Prevention Programs Try to Rein in Heroin, Pill Epidemic."
73. DeAnna DeCaluwe, "The Fly Effect, Marketing Campaign Review," Creative Communication & Design, October 9, 2013. www.creativecommunication.com.
74. Julie, *The Fly Effect*, September 2013. www.youtube.com.
75. Eric Holder, "Thanks to PERF for Bringing Us Together to Address the Heroin Epidemic," in *Subject to Debate*, March/April 2014. www.policeforum.org.

List of Illustrations

List of Illustrations

Index

Note: Boldface page numbers indicate illustrations.

Above the Influence, 35
abscesses, 35–36
Adams, Taite, 28, 49
addiction
    health risks of, 18
    to heroin vs. morphine, 29
    likelihood of, from heroin use, 8, 11–12
    overcoming, 9, 19–20
    prevalence of, 41
    signs of, 16, 18
    See also prevention/prevention programs; treatment
Alvarez, Manny, 21, 71
Associated Press, 23, 24, 47, 59, 60, 62
Association for Addiction Professionals (NAADAC), 54

Baler, Ruben, 19
black tar heroin, 12
brain
    addiction and, 12, 44
    effects of heroin on, 38–39, 44
    mechanism by which heroin affects, 15–16
Brownfield, William, 73
buprenorphine, 51, **60**
Burke, Kathleen M., 67
Business Insider (magazine), 53–54

Capretto, Neil, 21

Centers for Disease Control and Prevention (CDC), 38, 45
Central City Concern, 54–55
Cicero, Theodore J., 22–23
Cimons, Ben, 10–11
Comey, James B., 15, 21
Condon, Timothy P., 10, 44, 58, 63
Confront the Elephant program, 67–68

deaths
    from hepatitis C, 37
    from heroin overdose
        increase in, 22, 30, 32
        in Maryland, 46
        in Minnesota, 33
        reasons for, 18–19
        by state, **47**
        in Vermont, 26
    from tainted heroin, 48
DeCaluwe, DeAnna, 68
Department of Health and Human Services, US, 31, 37
Donnelly, Margaret T., 60
dopamine, 16
Douglas, Dan, 25
Drexler, Karen, 39–40
Drug Enforcement Administration (DEA), 15, 30, 34, 43
Drug Policy Alliance, 73, 74

Eisen, Lauren-Brooke, 64, 70

Picture Credits

About the Author

Peggy J. Parks holds a bachelor of science degree from Aquinas College in Grand Rapids, Michigan, where she graduated magna cum laude. An author who has written more than a hundred educational books for children and young adults, Parks lives in Muskegon, Michigan, a town that she says inspires her writing because of its location on the shores of Lake Michigan.